RECREATION

HAVING A GOOD
TIME IN AMERICA

W9-CZU-225

RECREATION

HAVING A GOOD TIME IN AMERICA

Mike Wilson

INFORMATION PLUS® REFERENCE SERIES
Formerly published by Information Plus, Wylie, Texas

Detroit
New York
San Francisco
London
Boston
Woodbridge, CT

RECREATION: HAVING A GOOD TIME IN AMERICA

Mike Wilson, *Author*

The Gale Group Staff:

Editorial: John F. McCoy, *Project Manager and Series Editor*; Andrew Claps, *Series Associate Editor*; Jason M. Everett, *Series Associate Editor*; Michael T. Reade, *Series Associate Editor*; Rita Runchock, *Managing Editor*; Luann Brennan, *Editor*

Image and Multimedia Content: Barbara J. Yarrow, *Manager, Imaging and Multimedia Content*; Robyn Young, *Project Manager, Imaging and Multimedia Content*

Indexing: Lynne Maday, *Indexing Specialist*; Amy Suchowski, *Indexing Specialist*

Permissions: Ryan Thomason, *Permissions Specialist*; Maria Franklin, *Permissions Manager*

Product Design: Michelle DiMercurio, *Senior Art Director*; Kenn Zorn, *Product Design Manager*

Production: Evi Seoud, *Assistant Manager, Composition Purchasing and Electronic Prepress*; NeKita McKee, *Buyer*; Dorothy Maki, *Manufacturing Manager*

While every effort has been made to ensure the reliability of the information presented in this publication, Gale does not guarantee the accuracy of the data contained herein. Gale accepts no payment for listing; and inclusion in the publication of any organization, agency, institution, publication, service, or individual does not imply endorsement of the editors or publisher. Errors brought to the attention of the publisher and verified to the satisfaction of the publisher will be corrected in future editions.

This publication is a creative work fully protected by all applicable copyright laws, as well as by misappropriation, trade secret, unfair competition, and other applicable laws. The authors and editors of this work have added value to the underlying factual material herein through one or more of the following: unique and original selection, coordination expression, arrangement, and classification of the information.

All rights to the publication will be vigorously defended.

Copyright © 2001 by Gale Group, Inc.
27500 Drake Rd.
Farmington Hills, Michigan 48331-3535

All rights reserved including the right of reproduction in whole or in part in any form.
Gale Group and Design is a trademark used herein under license.

ISBN 0-7876-5103-6 (set)
ISBN 0-7876-5403-5 (this volume)
ISSN 1543-1593 (this volume)
Printed in the United States of America
10 9 8 7 6 5 4 3 2 1

790.0973
W695r
2001
cop. 2

TABLE OF CONTENTS

CHAPTER 1
How Americans Spend Their Time 1

This chapter focuses on the most popular ways in which Americans spend their free time, including reading, sports and fitness, and personal computing.

CHAPTER 2
The Cost of Having Fun 13

Having fun can be expensive, and profitable. The increasing cost of recreation is discussed, as are sales trends for different segments of the recreation market, including sporting goods, consumer electronics, books, and toys.

CHAPTER 3
Outdoor Recreation 25

This chapter explores Americans' enduring love for the outdoors. It discusses the most popular forms of outdoor recreation; who participates, and why; the financial and ecological costs of spending time outdoors; and newer forms of outdoor recreation, such as extreme sports.

CHAPTER 4
The Arts and Media 41

Americans spend billions of dollars each year on art- and media-related activities, such as going to movies, attending concerts, and buying music and consumer electronics. This chapter explores how, where, and why. It also details trends in movie attendance, Internet use, record buying, and sales of televisions and other home electronics.

CHAPTER 5
Football, Baseball, Basketball, and Other Popular Sports . . 51

This chapter focuses on participation and attendance trends in different individual and team sports, including the "holy trinity" of American sports—baseball, basketball, and football—and many others, such as soccer, swimming, golf, and bowling. Gender- and race-related differences in participation are also discussed here.

CHAPTER 6
Gambling in America 57

The history of gambling in the United States is as old as the country itself. This chapter traces gambling's history in America, from its humble beginnings in the late 1700s to the multibillion-dollar industry it has become today, focusing on general trends and the many different types of gambling.

CHAPTER 7
Vacations and Travel. 73

People's destinations and means of travel may vary, but one thing is clear: Americans love to travel. Discussed here are Americans' reasons for traveling; different types of trips, including weekend excursions, adventure getaways, and heritage tourism; and trends in each type of travel.

CHAPTER 8
The Role of Recreation in American Society 87

As American society has changed, so too has the role of recreation. As this chapter illustrates, recreation today serves many functions, such as building physical and emotional well-being, and offering opportunities for socialization, as well as generating substantial profits. This chapter also explores several important aspects of recreation in America, including the commercialization of professional sports and the perceived "deification" of many professional athletes.

PREFACE

Recreation: Having a Good Time in America is the latest volume in the ever-growing *Information Plus Reference Series*. Previously published by the Information Plus company of Wylie, Texas, the *Information Plus Reference Series* (and its companion set, the *Information Plus Compact Series*) became a Gale Group product when Gale and Information Plus merged in early 2000. Those of you familiar with the series as published by Information Plus will notice a few changes from the 1999 edition. Gale has adopted a new layout and style that we hope you will find easy to use. Other improvements include greatly expanded indexes in each book, and more descriptive tables of contents.

While some changes have been made to the design, the purpose of the *Information Plus Reference Series* remains the same. Each volume of the series presents the latest facts on a topic of pressing concern in modern American life. These topics include today's most controversial and most studied social issues: abortion, capital punishment, care for the elderly, crime, health care, the environment, immigration, minorities, social welfare, women, youth, and many more. Although written especially for the high school and undergraduate student, this series is an excellent resource for anyone in need of factual information on current affairs.

By presenting the facts, it is Gale's intention to provide its readers with everything they need to reach an informed opinion on current issues. To that end, there is a particular emphasis in this series on the presentation of scientific studies, surveys, and statistics. This data is generally presented in the form of tables, charts, and other graphics placed within the text of each book. Every graphic is directly referred to and carefully explained in the text. The source of each graphic is presented within the graphic itself. The data used in these graphics is drawn from the most reputable and reliable sources, in particular from the various branches of the U.S. government and from major independent polling organizations. Every effort was made to secure the most recent information available. The reader should bear in mind that many major studies take years to conduct, and that additional years often pass before the data from these studies is made available to the public. Therefore, in many cases the most recent information available in 2001 dated from 1998 or 1999. Older statistics are sometimes presented as well, if they are of particular interest and no more-recent information exists.

Although statistics are a major focus of the *Information Plus Reference Series* they are by no means its only content. Each book also presents the widely held positions and important ideas that shape how the book's subject is discussed in the United States. These positions are explained in detail and, where possible, in the words of those who support them. Some of the other material to be found in these books includes: historical background; descriptions of major events related to the subject; relevant laws and court cases; and examples of how these issues play out in American life. Some books also feature primary documents, or have pro and con debate sections giving the words and opinions of prominent Americans on both sides of a controversial topic. All material is presented in an even-handed and unbiased manner; the reader will never be encouraged to accept one view of an issue over another.

HOW TO USE THIS BOOK

Everyone has a favorite activity or two that they enjoy doing in their free time, however much, or little, free time they have available. Almost all Americans enjoy watching television, reading, and spending time with friends, but beyond that their interests run in many directions. Some like to see movies, others prefer gambling. Many Americans enjoy sports, but while some like to play basketball, others just like to watch, or prefer "extreme" sports such as mountain biking or bungee jumping. A huge entertainment industry has developed in America to meet these varied needs. This book presents the latest information on America's leisure activities and compares it with years past to highlight trends in how Americans use their free time. Controversies over how entertainment activities may be hurting society, such as violence in the media, gambling, and the commercialization of sports, are explored.

Recreation: Having a Good Time in America consists of eight chapters and three appendices. Each chapter is devoted to a particular aspect of recreation in the United States. For a summary of the information covered in each chapter, please see the synopses provided in the Table of Contents at the front of the book. Chapters generally begin with an overview of the basic facts and background information on the chapter's topic, then proceed to examine sub-topics of particular interest. For example, Chapter 5: Football, Baseball, Basketball, and Other Popular Sports begins with an overview of the most popular spectator and participatory sports in the United States. Differences between male and female sports enthusiasts are highlighted. The chapter then proceeds into more detailed examinations of some of the most popular participatory sports, including basketball, soccer, and bowling. Readers can find their way through a chapter by looking for the section and sub-section headings, which are clearly set off from the text. Or, they can refer to the book's extensive index, if they already know what they are looking for.

Statistical Information

The tables and figures featured throughout *Recreation: Having a Good Time in America* will be of particular use to the reader in learning about this topic. These tables and figures represent an extensive collection of the most recent and valuable statistics on recreation and leisure; for example: how much Americans spend on different types of leisure activities, the number of Americans who gamble, the differences in the favorite leisure activities of Americans based on sex and income, and the impact of computers on recreation. Gale believes that making this information available to the reader is the most

important way in which we fulfill the goal of this book: To help readers understand the topic of recreation and reach their own conclusions about controversial issues related to entertainment in the United States.

Each table or figure has a unique identifier appearing above it, for ease of identification and reference. Titles for the tables and figures explain their purpose. At the end of each table or figure, the original source of the data is provided.

In order to help readers understand these often complicated statistics, all tables and figures are explained in the text. References in the text direct the reader to the relevant statistics. Furthermore, the contents of all tables and figures are fully indexed. Please see the opening section of the index at the back of this volume for a description of how to find tables and figures within it.

In addition to the main body text and images, *Recreation: Having a Good Time in America* has three appendices. The first is the Important Names and Addresses directory. Here the reader will find contact information for a number of organizations that study recreation. The second appendix is the Resources section, which is provided to assist the reader in conducting his or her own research. In this section, the author and editors of *Recreation: Having a Good Time in America* describe some of the sources that were most useful during the compilation of this book. The final appendix is this book's index. It has been greatly expanded from previous editions, and should make it even easier to find specific topics in this book.

COMMENTS AND SUGGESTIONS

The editor of the *Information Plus Reference Series* welcomes your feedback on *Recreation: Having a Good Time in America*. Please direct all correspondence to:

Editor
Information Plus Reference Series
27500 Drake Rd.
Farmington Hills, MI, 48331-3535

ACKNOWLEDGEMENTS

The editors wish to thank the copyright holders of the excerpted material included in this volume and the permissions managers of many book and magazine publishing companies for assisting us in securing reproduction rights. We are also grateful to the staffs of the Detroit Public Library, the Library of Congress, the University of Detroit Mercy Library, Wayne State University Purdy/Kresge Library Complex, and the University of Michigan Libraries for making their resources available to us. Following is a list of the copyright holders who have granted us permission to reproduce material in this volume of Recreation: Having a Good Time in America. Every effort has been made to trace copyright, but if omissions have been made, please let us know.

COPYRIGHTED MATERIAL IN RECREATION: HAVING A GOOD TIME IN AMERICA WAS REPRODUCED FROM THE FOLLOWING SOURCES:

From a report prepared by American Booksellers Association Research Department. Copyright © 1999 American Booksellers Association. Reproduced by permission.

From a study in *Pari-Mutuel Racing—1996.* Copyright © 1996 Association of Racing Commissioners International, Inc. Reproduced by permission.

From a study in *Book Industry Trends 1999.* Copyright © 1999 Book Industry Study Group. Reproduced by permission.

From a study in *International Gaming & Wagering Business, August 1997 Supplement.* Copyright © 1997 BPI International. Reproduced by permission.

From a study in *International Gaming & Wagering Business, August 1998 Supplement.* Copyright © 1998 BPI International. Reproduced by permission.

From a study in *Consumer Electronics and the U.S. Economy.* Copyright © Consumer Electronics Association. Reproduced by permission.

From a study in *Poll Release,* March 1, 1999. Copyright © 1999 The Gallup Organization. Reproduced by permission.

From a study in *The Gallup Poll Monthly,* July, 1996; 1997; July 8, 1999; January 4, 2000; April, 2000; August 31, 2000. Copyright © 2000 The Gallup Organization. All reproduced by permission.

From a study by The Gallup Organization. Copyright © The Gallup Organization. Reproduced by permission.

From a study in *The HIA Nationwide Craft/Hobby Consumer Study.* Copyright © 1999 Hobby Industry Association. Reproduced by permission.

From a study in *1996–97 Size of Craft/Hobby Industry.* Copyright © Hobby Industry Association. Reproduced by permission.

From a study in *America's Senior Volunteers.* Copyright © by Independent Sector. Reproduced by permission.

From a study in *Giving and Volunteering in the United States.* Copyright © 1999 by Independent Sector. Reproduced by permission.

From a study by Leisure Trends Group. Copyright © Leisure Trends Group. Reproduced by permission.

From a study by NFO Research, Inc. Copyright © 1997 Harrah's Entertainment, Inc. Reproduced by permission.

From a study by NFO Research, Inc. and the U.S. Census Bureau. Copyright © 1997 Harrah's Entertainment, Inc. Reproduced by permission.

From a study by NPD Group. Copyright © NPD Group, Inc.

From a study in *Pew Research Center Biennal News Consumption Survey.* Copyright © 1998 The Pew Research Center. Reproduced by permission.

From a study by Recording Industry Association of America. Copyright © Recording Industry Association of America. Reproduced by permission.

From a study by Recreational Vehicle Industry Association. Copyright © Recreational Vehicle Industry Association. Reproduced by permission.

From a study in *Outdoor Recreation in America 1999: The Family and the Environment.* Copyright © 1999 Roper Starch. Reproduced by permission.

From a study in *Spreadsheets to Sunshine: Executives on Vacation.* Copyright © 1998 Roper Starch Worldwide, Inc. Reproduced by permission.

From a study by Sporting Goods Manufacturer's Association, May, 2000; June, 2000; July 26, 2000; July 31, 2000; August, 2000; August 28, 2000; October 30, 2000; November, 2000. Copyright © 2000 Sporting Goods Manufacturer's Association. All reproduced by permission.

From a study in *The U.S. Athletic Footwear Market Today, 1998 Edition.* Copyright © 1998 by Sporting Goods Manufacturers Association. Reproduced by permission.

From a study in *Sports Participation Trends Report, 1997.* Copyright © 1998 Sporting Goods Manufacturers Association. Reproduced by permission.

From a study in *America's Favorite Team Sport.* Copyright © 1997 by Sporting Goods Manufacturers Association. Reproduced by permission. From a study by Soccer Industry

Council of America. Copyright Sporting Goods Manufacturers Association. Reproduced by permission.

From a report by Stanford Institute for the Quantitative Study of Society. Copyright © 2000 Stanford Institute for the Quantitative Study of Society, Stanford University. Reproduced by permission.

From a study by Toy Manufacturers Association. Copyright © Toy Manufacturers of America. Reproduced by permission.

From a study by Travel Industry Association of America. Copyright © 1999 Travel Industry Association of America. Reproduced by permission.

From a study by Travelscope. Copyright © Travel Industry Association of America. Reproduced by permission.

From a study in *TIA Travel Poll,* June 12, 2000; July 7, 2000. Copyright © 2000 Travel Industry Association of America. Both reproduced by permission.

From a study by Travel Industry Association of America. Copyright © 1998 Travel Industry Association of America. Reproduced by permission.

CHAPTER 1
HOW AMERICANS SPEND THEIR TIME

DEFINING LEISURE AND RECREATION

The word "leisure" comes from the Latin word *licere,* which means "to be allowed." Most Americans view leisure as something allowed after one's work is done: time free after required activities. Recreation, however, is a different matter. The *Oxford American Dictionary* defines recreation as "a process or means of refreshing or entertaining oneself after work by some pleasurable activity." Its Latin and French roots, which mean "restore to health" or "create anew," imply refreshment of strength or spirit. While leisure activities are pastimes, recreational activities are intended to restore physical or mental health.

HOW MUCH FREE TIME?

By most international comparisons, Americans enjoy one of the highest standards of living in the world. And although many people express serious concerns about the United States, the world generally respects—even envies—the quality of life enjoyed by most Americans.

Americans do work hard. Although there has been no significant change since the 1970s in the number of hours of nonwork time available to Americans, surveys consistently report that Americans believe they have less free time today than in the past. Many people feel they are almost always in a rush and under stress. Many report they do not get enough sleep each day, and most believe they do not have sufficient time for family and pleasurable activities. Some even label themselves workaholics. Others believe they have filled their leisure hours with so much activity that it also becomes stressful, not "re-creating."

A PERSONAL CHOICE

People who perform certain activities all day at a job often like to do different things on their time off. Someone who sits behind a desk at work may choose to do some-

TABLE 1.1

Top 10 favorite activities for 1998

- Reading 35.8%
- Television 24.8%
- Time w/family/friends 18.7%
- Movies 10.8%
- Walking 10.2%
- Shopping 10.2%
- Fishing 8.7%
- Listening to radio 8.5%
- Sewing & knitting 7.2%
- Gardening 6.9%

SOURCE: Leisure Trends Group, Boulder, CO, no date

thing physically active, such as recreational walking, the most popular participatory sport among both women and men during 1999 (see Chapter 5). A person with a job that requires physical work may choose a more sedentary activity, such as computer games, reading, or painting. A person who lives in a flat region may go to the mountains to seek excitement, while someone living in the mountains might seek out a sandy ocean beach on which to relax.

Other people may enjoy one field so much that they perform that activity not only professionally, but also as a form of recreation. Some observers have suggested that, as many Americans derive less satisfaction from jobs where they have little input, recreation becomes even more important to a happy life. (For more discussion of the role recreation plays in American society, see Chapter 8.)

HOW DO AMERICANS LIKE TO SPEND THEIR LEISURE TIME?

A 1998 survey conducted by the Leisure Trends Group found that more than one-third of Americans said that reading was their favorite way to spend leisure time. (See Table 1.1.) Despite these claims, survey results indicated that Americans were, in practice, more likely to

TABLE 1.2

Top 10 leisure activities for 1998

- Television 34.2%
- Reading 16.4%
- Shopping 11.3%
- Time w/family/friends 8.9%
- Rest/relaxation 6.2%
- House cleaning 5.8%
- Spectator sports 5.1%
- Movies 4.4%
- Walking 4.3%
- Eating-out 4.2%

SOURCE: Leisure Trends Group, Boulder, CO, no date

TABLE 1.3

What is your favorite way to spend an evening?

1. Watching television	31%
2. Being with family, husband, wife	20%
3. Reading	18%
4. Dining out	15%
5. Going to movies or theater	11%
6. Resting or relaxing	10%
7. Watching movies at home	7%
8. Visiting friends or relatives	6%
9. Entertaining friends or relatives	5%
10. Listening to music	4%

Note: Total adds to more than 100% due to multiple responses

SOURCE: *Poll Release,* Gallup Organization, March 1, 1999

watch television as to read. (See Table 1.2.) Indeed, a 1999 Gallup survey showed that twice as many Americans chose watching television rather than reading when asked their favorite way to spend an evening. (See Table 1.3.)

Also, reading is apparently more popular among women than men. A 1999 Gallup poll found that 64 percent of women reported reading six or more books during the year, but only 42 percent of men had done so.

Other favorite ways to spend leisure time were spending time with family and friends (18.7 percent), seeing a movie (10.8 percent), walking (10.2 percent), shopping (10.2 percent), fishing (8.7 percent), listening to the radio (8.5 percent), sewing and knitting (7.2 percent), and gardening (6.9 percent).

A comparison of how leisure time is spent versus what Americans say are their favorite ways to spend leisure time suggests that they do not always get to spend their leisure time in ways that they like. For example, housecleaning ranked sixth in the top 10 leisure activities but did not rank at all among the top 10 favorite activities!

HOW AMERICANS RELAX

Most Americans live busy lives with little time to relax. A survey of one thousand adults, taken by the Dial Corporation in 1995, revealed how they used that time. Taking a warm bath or shower was America's favorite way to relax, although more women than men liked to relax this way. Of the women surveyed, 54 percent liked to soak in the tub, compared with 39 percent of men. (See Figure 1.1.)

Exercising (48 percent) was the favorite way to unwind for men, followed by sex (40 percent). Of the men surveyed, 32 percent had a drink to relax. Having a drink (22 percent) or sex (18 percent) were the least favorite ways to relax for women. Women were twice as likely to call a friend (42 percent), go shopping (38 percent), or eat (32 percent). For men, going shopping (22 percent) was their least favorite way to relax.

FAVORITE WAYS TO SPEND AN EVENING

A 1999 Gallup survey found that Americans' favorite way to spend an evening was watching television (31 percent). (See Table 1.3.) Other favorite ways of spending an evening included being with one's family or spouse (20 percent), reading (18 percent), dining out (15 percent), and going to the movies or theater (11 percent).

Interestingly, television has been the most popular way for Americans to spend an evening since 1960, based upon previous Gallup polls that asked this same question.

WHEN THEY ARE ALONE

Americans often find themselves alone. What do they do with that time? Roper Starch Worldwide, in a 1997 survey, found that, for men, watching television was the favorite way to spend solitary time (37 percent). For women, 50 percent cooked when they were alone (this likely does not indicate a preference for cooking as a hobby but, rather, the necessity of cooking for the family, even when they were not present).

Reading books was the second-most common solitary activity for both men (33 percent) and women (43 percent). For men, in third place came watching sports (30 percent), followed by home repairs (27 percent), napping (26 percent), cooking (22 percent), and browsing in stores (11 percent). In third place for women was watching television (35 percent), followed by napping (33 percent), browsing in stores (24 percent), and home repairs and watching sports (8 percent each). Only 5 percent of men or women frequently ate out in restaurants, and only 3 percent often went to movies or took weekend trips by themselves.

FIGURE 1.1

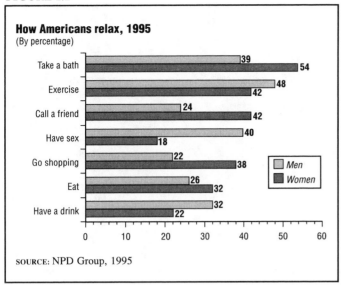

How Americans relax, 1995
(By percentage)

SOURCE: NPD Group, 1995

READING

Reading is one of the favorite leisure activities among Americans. According to figures provided by the American Booksellers Association, consumers spent $1.72 billion on children's books and $4.8 billion on adult books during 1999. Many other people checked out books from libraries, purchased used books, and passed books to friends or family.

According to figures of the American Booksellers Association, the total number of adult books sold remained nearly flat in 1999, but the children's book market experienced a dramatic increase, with sales of paperbacks increasing 23.5 percent and sales of hardcover books increasing by 11.1 percent. The *Harry Potter* children's books were responsible for much of this increase.

During 1999 adult trade paperback sales increased by 3.2 percent, after larger increases of 10.2 percent in 1998 and 7.5 percent in 1997, according to the American Booksellers Association. Sales of hardcovers grew only 2.6 percent. Experts attributed the slow growth in sales to the high price of hardcover books. There also has been a major shift, described in Chapter 2, in the way consumers purchase books. Increasingly, purchases are being made on the Internet rather than at bookstores. In late 1999 over 22 million American adults were shopping for books online according the American Booksellers Association.

Who Reads What?

According to a 1999 Gallup poll, Americans preferred to read nonfiction. Of the Americans polled by Gallup, 46 percent said they read primarily nonfiction. Another 35 percent read mostly fiction, and 17 percent said they read both fiction and nonfiction equally. Among men, 51 percent said they preferred nonfiction while only 41 percent of women said they preferred nonfiction.

A study based on data collected by NPD Group, a major marketing research firm, and published in a report prepared by the American Booksellers Association Research Department, estimated the top selling adult books by category. In 1998 over half of adult books sold were popular fiction (51.9 percent). (See Table 1.4.) The study showed that the market share of popular fiction remained within a few percentage points of 50 percent from 1995 through 1998.

In 1998 the next most popular categories of book sales were cooking/crafts, with a 10.1 percent market share, and religion, with a 9.9 percent market share. No other category came close to claiming a 10 percent market share. General nonfiction books, however, made up 8.2 percent of the total number of books sold. Books on psychology/self-help (6.3 percent) and books that were technical, scientific, or educational (5.8 percent) were the only other categories exceeding 5 percent in market share.

In general, America's taste in books, as measured by market share, did not change much from 1995 to 1998. The same study, however, also collected share information by category for book purchases as far back as 1991. Comparing market share figures from 1991 to 1998, researchers found one category that had more than doubled in market share: Religious books were 4.7 percent of the books sold in 1991. By 1998 the market share of religious books had grown to 9.9 percent.

COMPUTERS IN DAILY HOME USE

Personal computing has become an important leisure activity. The cost of buying a computer decreased significantly in the 1990s, and the growing affordability increased computer ownership. There are many different kinds of software available, such as games, financial programs, programs that teach foreign languages, and others that search the Internet. As of 1996, half of American public schools had access to the Internet. Of the schools with access to the World Wide Web, 70 percent of the students had the ability to use it. The 1998 National Survey of Public Library Outlets with Internet Connectivity found that 84 percent of suburban libraries provided Internet access to the public and 68 percent of rural libraries did so.

The Consumer Electronics Manufacturers Association (now called the Consumer Electronics Association) reported, in *Internet and Multimedia PC Usage,* that, in 1998, multimedia personal computer (PC) users also used their computers for other purposes: 55 percent of households with PCs owned more than 15 CD-ROMs, and 71 percent used their CD-ROM drives to play audio CDs. One-fourth had listened to live radio broadcasts with their computers.

Internet Use Is Becoming the Norm

In 1998 an estimated 22 percent of the American public had accessed the Internet in the previous month.

TABLE 1.4

Category share of consumer purchases of adult books 1995–98*

	1998		1997		1996		1995	
	UNITS (000's)	%	UNITS (000's)	%	UNITS (000's)	%	UNITS (000's)	%
Total Categories	1,015,0763	100.0	1,067,015	100.0	1,060,251	100.0	1,027,716	100.0
Popular Fiction	527,211	51.9	537,296	50.4	539,265	50.9	513,849	50.0
General Non-Fiction	83,608	8.2	95,019	8.9	99,911	9.4	95,243	9.3
Cooking/Crafts	102,206	10.1	108,508	10.2	107,634	10.2	116,132	11.3
Psychology/Recovery	63,834	6.3	67,043	6.3	65,272	6.2	61,786	6.0
Religious	100,295	9.9	91,627	8.6	78,025	7.4	74,797	7.3
Technical/Science/Education	59,419	5.8	59,676	5.6	59,354	5.6	56,811	5.5
Art/Literature/Poetry	39,231	3.9	39,963	3.7	42,535	4.0	39,303	3.8
Reference	25,626	2.5	28,100	2.6	23,938	2.3	26,688	2.6
Travel/Regional	14,332	1.4	13,469	1.3	14,563	1.4	15,478	1.5

* Excludes Alaska and Hawaii

1. Popular Fiction includes Adult, Espionage/Thriller, Fantasy, General, Historical, Male Adventure, Mystery/Detective, Occult, Religious, Romance, Science Fiction, Suspense/Psychology, TV Movies & Western.

2. General Non-Fiction includes Biography/Autobiography, Non-Fiction Crime/True Adventure, Non-Fiction - General, Humor/Jokes, History - Military/War & Histor

3. Cooking/Crafts includes Animals, Antiques/Collectibles, Photography, Automotive, Crafts/Hobbies, Cooking/Wine, Do-it-Yourself/Home Improvement, Gardening/Indoor Plants, Nature/Guidebooks, Transportation & Sports/Recreation.

4. Psychology/Recovery includes Psychology/Pop Psychology, Childbirth/Childcare/Family, Love/Sex/Marriage, Diet/Health/Exercise, Grooming and Recovery.   y - General.

5. Religious includes Inspirational, New Age, Philosophy - Eastern Religious, Theology, Bibles/Prayer Books, Religion - Biblical Studies, Religion - Christian Education, Religion - Christian Living, Religion - Church Administration, Religion/Judaism, Religion - Issues, Religion - History, Religion - Missions, Religion - Family, Religion - Worship, Religion - Devotions, Religion - Classics, Religion Roman Catholic, Religion - World Religions, Religion - Youth Ministries & Religion - Reference/Study Guide.

6. Technical/Science/Education includes Business/Economics, Technical, Education, Medical, Science/Mathematics, Sociology/Anthropology/Archeology, Environmental Studies & Computer Books.

7. Art/Literature/Poetry includes Art/Architecture, Literature - Classics/Contemporary, Performing Arts, Poetry/Plays & Pop Arts.

8. Reference includes Cliff/Monarch Notes, Study Guides & Reference.

9. Travel/Regional includes Travel - General, Travel - Domestic, Travel - Foreign, Regional Interest - Central, Regional Interest - East & Regional Interest - West.

10. As of 1998 a tenth category "All Other Categories" was reorganized into the other categories.

SOURCE: Report prepared by American Booksellers Association Research Department. Data collected and tabulated by NPD Group, 1999

Mediamark Research, a New York survey organization, found that one-fourth of men and one-fifth of women had done so. The higher the income, the more likely a person was to have used the Internet, with 6 percent of those making less than $10,000 and 38 percent of those making $50,000 or more accessing the Internet. The more education, the more likely that person was to get online; 7 percent of those without a high school diploma and 49 percent of college graduates used the service. Approximately 27 percent of those 18–54 accessed the Internet, compared with 13 percent of those 55 and older and just 3 percent of those over 65.

Use of the Internet continues to grow dramatically. A 1999 study by Media Research found that 64 million American adults, or nearly one-third of the population over 18 years of age, were using the Internet at least once a month. Another study using statistics from IntelliQuest found that 83 million, or 40 percent of persons in America over 16 years of age, were using the Internet in 1999.

The Pew Research Center for the People and the Press, in *The Internet News Audience Goes Ordinary* (1999), reported that the Internet audience is not only growing, but is increasingly resembling the population as a whole. (See Chapter 4, however, for a discussion of demographic differences in Internet access and use.) Whereas well-educated, affluent men were once the great-est users of the Internet, people without college training, those with modest incomes, and women are using the Internet more and more. Fully 39 percent of those who started going online in the year before the study never attended college, compared with 22 percent of experienced Internet users. Similarly, 23 percent of new users had household incomes below $30,000, compared with 16 percent of experienced users.

The study found that Internet news interests were changing: weather and entertainment were growing faster than political and international news. The majority of the online public (85 percent) used electronic mail (e-mail). E-mail use has also changed dramatically, with 88 percent of those using it either for personal use exclusively (41 percent) or for a combination of personal and work communication (47 percent) in 1998. In 1995, 31 percent of those online used e-mail exclusively for business.

Most Internet users with e-mail (61 percent) checked their e-mail every day; 20 percent, every other day; and 14 percent, once a week. The average user sent eight e-mails per week. When not e-mailing, Internet users accessed information or played online games.

Youths, Teens, and College Students on the Internet

Almost half of all American children between the ages of 2 and 12 were projected to be online by 2002,

FIGURE 1.2

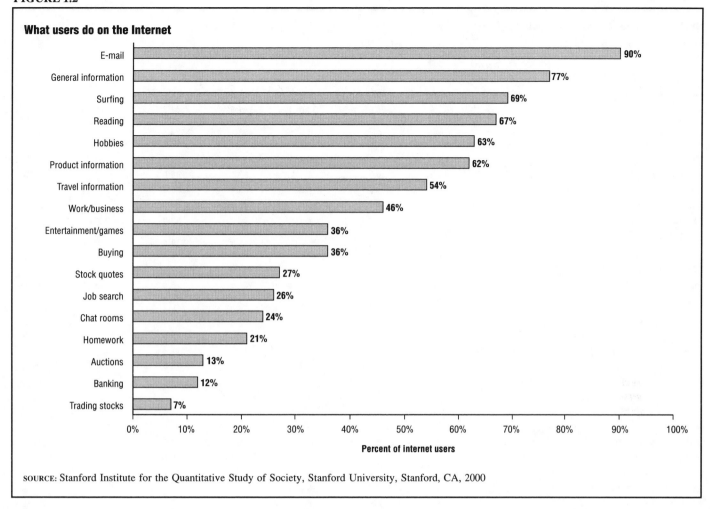

What users do on the Internet

Activity	Percent
E-mail	90%
General information	77%
Surfing	69%
Reading	67%
Hobbies	63%
Product information	62%
Travel information	54%
Work/business	46%
Entertainment/games	36%
Buying	36%
Stock quotes	27%
Job search	26%
Chat rooms	24%
Homework	21%
Auctions	13%
Banking	12%
Trading stocks	7%

Percent of internet users

SOURCE: Stanford Institute for the Quantitative Study of Society, Stanford University, Stanford, CA, 2000

according to the *1998 Jupiter Communications Consumer Content Report*. It was estimated that 18.8 million children under 18 had access to home computers. Teens spent an average of 8.5 hours a week chatting and e-mailing on the Internet, and about 1.8 hours a week for school work.

According to a January 1999 survey conducted by the American Council on Education and the Graduate School of Education and Information Studies at the University of California at Los Angeles, college students were frequent users of the Internet. At American colleges, 83 percent of freshmen reported using the Internet for research and homework. Nearly two-thirds of the students at two-year and four-year colleges who responded to the survey said that they used the Internet to communicate by e-mail.

Computer Use among Those 45 and Older

The American Association of Retired Persons found, in 1999, that senior citizens were the fastest-growing segment of Internet users. Of those aged 45 and older, 81 percent had access to the Internet. They spent an average of five hours per week on e-mail activities and about nine hours per week on other activities. About half of Internet users aged 45 and older used the Internet for comparison shopping and 39 percent made purchases over the Internet.

Computer users 45 and older had had their computers for an average of 8.5 years and had been accessing the Internet for an average of 3.3 years.

Activities on the Internet

The Stanford Institute for the Qualitative Study of Society, at Stanford University, published a study in 1999 that reported the types of activities engaged in by Internet users. The study found that e-mail was the most popular activity, with 90 percent of all Internet users reporting that they used e-mail. (See Figure 1.2.) Researchers found that Americans were using the Internet as a giant informational search utility to obtain general information as well as specific information about hobbies (63 percent) and products (62 percent). Information about travel was sought by 54 percent of Internet users, and over a quarter (27 percent) used the Internet to check stock prices.

Almost half of Internet users (46 percent) used the Internet for work and business purposes. Searching for jobs on the Internet attracted 26 percent of users; 21 percent used the Internet for homework.

TABLE 1.5

Fitness participation trends in detail

(Millions of Americans aged 6 and older)

[ ] = Average days of participation, 1999	1987	1990	1993	1997	1998	1999	Change: 98-99	Change: 87 -99
Free weights	22.6	26.7	28.6	39.8	41.3	**42.8**	+ 3.6%	+ 89.4%
Barbells [95]	n.a.	n.a.	n.a.	n.a.	21.3	**21.7**	+ 1.9%*	n.a.
Dumbbells [92]	n.a.	n.a.	n.a.	n.a.	23.4	**24.8**	+ 6.0%	n.a.
Hand weights [84]	n.a.	n.a.	n.a.	n.a.	23.3	**25.9**	+11.2%	n.a.
Treadmill [63]	4.4	11.5	19.7	36.1	37.1	**37.5**	+ 1.1%*	+ 752%
Fitness walking [116]	27.2	37.4	36.3	38.8	36.4	**36.0**	- 1.1%*	+32.4%
Stretching [117]	n.a.	n.a.	n.a	n.a	35.1	**35.3**	+ 0.6%*	n.a.
Running/jogging [79]	37.1	35.7	34.1	36.5	35.0	**34.0**	- 2.9%*	- 8.4%
Stationary cycling	30.8	39.8	36.0	32.0	30.8	**30.9**	+ 0.3%*	+ 0.3%*
Upright bikes [62]	n.a.	n.a.	n.a.	n.a.	20.7	**18.3**	-11.6%	n.a.
Recumbent bikes [63]	n.a.	n.a.	n.a.	n.a.	6.8	**9.8**	+44.1%	n.a.
Group cycling [52]	n.a.	n.a.	n.a.	n.a.	6.8	**6.9**	+ 1.5%*	n.a.
Calisthenics [104]	n.a.	n.a.	n.a.	n.a.	31.0	**27.5**	-11.3%	n.a.
Resistance machines [78]	15.3	16.8	19.4	22.5	22.5	**23.0**	+ 2.2%*	+50.3%
Aerobic dance	21.2	23.0	24.8	22.8	21.0	**19.1**	- 4.3%	- 9.9%
High-impact [67]	14.0	12.4	10.4	10.2	7.5	**6.2**	-17.3%	-55.7%
Low-impact [58]	11.9	16.0	13.4	11.2	12.8	**11.6**	- 9.4%	- 2.5%*
Step [52]	n.a.	n.a.	11.5	10.8	10.8	**9.5**	-12.0%	-17.4%[1]
Abdominal trainer [76]	n.a.	n.a.	n.a.	n.a.	16.5	**17.1**	+ 3.6%*	n.a.
Stair-climbing machines [54]	2.1	13.5	22.5	17.9	18.6	**16.3**	-12.4%	+676%
Fitness swimming [49]	16.9	18.0	17.5	16.2	15.3	**14.2**	- 7.2%*	-16.0%
Other exercise to music [65]	n.a.	n.a.	n.a.	n.a.	13.8	**12.9**	- 6.5%*	n.a.
Fitness bicycling [58]	n.a.	n.a.	n.a.	n.a.	13.6	**12.3**	- 9.6%	n.a.
Home gym [81]	3.9	4.7	6.3	6.8	7.6	**7.9**	+ 3.9%*	+103%
Cardio kick-boxing [33]	n.a.	n.a.	n.a.	n.a.	n.a.	**7.6**	n.a.	n.a.
Yoga/Tai Chi [49]	n.a.	n.a.	n.a.	n.a.	5.7	**6.4**	+ 12.2%	n.a.
Rowing machine [47]	14.5	14.6	11.3	8.4	7.5	**6.3**	- 16.0%	-56.6%
Cross-country ski machine [57]	n.a.	6.4	9.8	8.9	6.9	**5.9**	- 14.4%	- 7.8%[2]
Water exercise [48]	n.a.	n.a.	n.a.	6.3	6.7	**5.6**	- 16.4%	-11.1%[3]
Elliptical motion trainer [61]	n.a.	n.a.	n.a.	2.4	3.9	**5.1**	+ 30.8%	+113%[3]
Aerobic rider [58]	n.a	n.a.	n.a.	8.6	5.9	**4.2**	-28.8%	-51.2%[3]

* Change is within sample parameters and is not statistically significant.
[1] Since 1993
[2] Since 1990
[3] Since 1997

SOURCE: "The Shifting Fashions in Exercise," Sporting Goods Manufacturer's Association, North Palm Beach, FL, November 2000

The Internet, however, is for play as well. More than one-third (36 percent) of Americans used the Internet for entertainment and to play games. Chat rooms drew the participation of 24 percent of Internet users. The institute found that chat-room activity was much more pronounced in users under age 25.

Internet users were beginning to use the Internet for commercial activities as well. The Internet was used for banking by 12 percent; 13 percent participated in online auctions; and 7 percent used the Internet to trade stocks.

FITNESS ACTIVITIES—AN IMPORTANT PART OF MANY LIVES

Like tastes in foods, fashions, and music, American exercise habits have undergone significant shifts. Fitness has become important to many Americans. The Sporting Goods Manufacturers Association (SGMA), in a 1999 report, set forth some interesting facts about Americans' preoccupation with fitness and trends in fitness activity:

- Nearly 31 million Americans had joined health clubs. This represented an increase of 48 percent from 1990. Health-club members were older, as well. In 1990, 39 percent of all health-club members were 35 or older. In 1999, 56 percent were 35 or older.

- The most popular type of fitness exercise was the use of free weights; 42.8 million Americans worked out with free weights in 1999. (See Table 1.5.)

- The second-most popular form of fitness exercise in 1999 was the use of treadmills. It also was the number-one fitness equipment purchase. Americans spent $1.6

TABLE 1.6

Top 30 most popular sports
(6 years of age or older; participated at least once in 1999)

Sport	# of Participants (millions)
1. Recreational swimming	95.1
2. Recreational walking	84.1
3. Recreational bicycling	56.2
4. Bowling	52.6
5. Freshwater fishing	44.5
6. Free weights	42.8
7. Tent camping	40.8
8. Basketball	39.4
9. Day hiking	39.2
10. Treadmill exercise	37.5
11. Billiards/pool	36.4
12. Fitness walking	36.0
13. Stretching	35.3
14. Running/jogging	34.0
15. Stationary cycling	31.0
16. Golf	28.2
17. In-line skating	27.9
18. Calisthenics	27.5
19. Weight/resistance machines	23.0
20. Darts	19.8
21. Volleyball (hard surface/grass)	19.1
21. Aerobics (high/low impact or step)	19.1
23. Slo-pitch softball	17.9
24. Soccer	17.6
24. RV camping	17.6
26. Ice skating	17.5
27. Abdominal machine	17.1
28. Horseback riding	16.9
29. Tennis	16.8
30. Touch football	16.7
30. Hunting (shotgun/rifle)	16.7

SOURCE: "SGMA Brings You America's Most Popular Sports," Sporting Goods Manufacturer's Association, North Palm Beach, FL, May 2000

TABLE 1.7

Number of participants who participated in sports "frequently"
(in thousands of people)

Activity	1998	1999	Percent change 98 - 99
Fitness	49,124	49,204	0.0%
Team sports	25,042	24,799	- 1.0%
Racquet sports	6,451	5,561	-13.8%
Recreational	30,928	28,757	- 7.0%
Outdoors	61,994	64,743	+ 4.4%
Winter	13,077	13,218	+ 1.1%
Water sports	5,288	3,313	-18.4%
Cardio equipment	17,279	17,288	0.0%
Strength equipment	18,920	20,424	+ 8.0%
Strength training	26,673	25,757	+ 0.3%
Cardio exercise	45,759	44,369	- 3.0%

SOURCE: "Avid Sports Participants Profiled in New Report," Sporting Goods Manufacturer's Association, North Palm Beach, FL, June 2000

AMERICA'S MOST POPULAR SPORTS

The SGMA determined the top 30 most popular sports in America based upon the number of participants. (See Table 1.6.) Recreational swimming had the most participants, with 95.1 million persons participating at least once during 1999. Not far behind in numbers of participants during 1999 was recreational walking with 84.1 million. Other popular sports in 1999 included recreational bicycling (56.2 million), bowling (52.6 million), freshwater fishing (44.5 million), free weights (42.8 million), and tent camping (40.8 million).

Another survey by the SGMA measured the change in the number of participants in sports who participated in those sports "frequently." The category having the greatest number of frequent participants was outdoor activities, with over 64 million. (See Table 1.7.) This category experienced an increase of 4.4 percent over figures for 1998. Close behind it were participants in fitness (49.2 million) and cardiovascular exercise (44.3 million). The category in which the greatest increase in frequent participation occurred was strength equipment (20.4 million), which experienced an increase of 8 percent over 1998 figures.

Popular Sports for Children and Seniors

America's love of sports and fitness is not bounded by age. The SGMA studied recreational activities that were "frequent" among youths ages 6–17 during 1999. The study found that American youth enjoy both team sports and individual sports, both fitness and recreation, and both indoor activities and outdoor activities.

The most popular frequent recreational activity for youth was recreational bicycle riding, with 11.4 million frequent participants. (See Table 1.8.) Close behind was basketball, with 10.7 million frequent participants. During 1999, 8.2 million youths swam frequently for recreation.

billion on treadmills in 1999. At the beginning of the 1990s, stationary bikes were the most popular cardiovascular machines. Treadmill exercise, however, rose from 11.5 million participants in 1990 to 37.5 million in 1999. In the late 1990s there was an increase in use of a new "no-impact" cardio machine, the elliptical cross-trainer. This machine attracted 5.1 million users in 1999, an increase of 31 percent over 1998.

- The use of resistance machines rose 50 percent during the 1990s to 23 million participants. The study found that personal trainers played a significant role in encouraging both men and women to use resistance training.

A 1997 report from American Sports Data found that Americans exercised for a variety of reasons. Men worked out mainly to improve muscle tone (84.7 percent), to increase energy (83 percent), for cardiovascular benefits (82 percent), and to control weight (82 percent). Women exercised mostly to control weight (88 percent), feel good (87 percent), increase energy (86 percent), and improve muscle tone (84 percent). Other reasons given by both sexes included increased flexibility, reduced stress, improved self-esteem, and time for self.

TABLE 1.8

Most popular sports for youth based on "frequent" participation
(Ages 6 - 17)

Activity	1999 (000)
1. Bicycling (recreational) - 52+ days/year	11,454
2. Basketball - 25+ days/year	10,702
3. Swimming (recreational) - 52+ days/year	8,244
4. In-line skating - 25+ days/year	6,992
5. Soccer - 25+ days/year	6,572
6. Baseball - 25+ days/year	5,261
7. Walking (recreational) - 52+ days/year	4,491
8. Calisthenics - 100+ days/year	3,720
9. Running/jogging - 100+ days/year	3,368
10. Football (touch) - 25+ days/year	3,345

SOURCE: "America's Children Like Diversity in their Activities," Sporting Goods Manufacturer's Association, North Palm Beach, FL, August 2000

TABLE 1.9

Most popular sports for seniors based on "frequent" participation
(Ages 55+)

Activity	1999 (000)
1. Walking (recreational) - 52+ days/year	9,647
2. Fitness walking - 100+ days/year	6,483
3. Stretching - 100+ days/year	3,228
4. Treadmill exercise - 100+ days/year	2,560
5. Golf - 25+ days/year	2,268
6. Bowling - 25+ days/year	2,114
7. Swimming (recreational) - 52+ days/year	1,952
8. Fishing (freshwater/other) - 15+ days/year	1,708
9. Free weights: hand weights - 100+ days/year	1,660
10. Camping (recreational vehicle) - 15+ days/year	1,552

SOURCE: "America's Seniors are no Couch Potatoes," Sporting Goods Manufacturer's Association, North Palm Beach, FL, August 2000

In-line skating and soccer were nearly tied in popularity as recreational activities engaged in frequently by youth. During 1999, 6.9 million youths frequently engaged in in-line skating and 6.5 million frequently played soccer.

America's seniors were frequent participants in recreational and fitness activity. SGMA's 1999 report found that 9.6 million seniors (aged 55 and over) engaged in recreational walking at least 52 days per year. (See Table 1.9.) An additional 6.4 million walked for fitness 100 or more days per year. Stretching and treadmill exercise were popular frequent activities for seniors, with 3.2 million and 2.5 million participants, respectively.

Retired Americans are often thought of as spending their leisure time playing golf. In fact, the SGMA survey supports this stereotype to some extent. During 1999, 2.2 million seniors played golf 25 days or more. Other popular frequent leisure activities for seniors included bowling (2.1 million), recreational swimming (1.9 million), fishing (1.7 million), working out with free weights (1.6 million), and camping (1.5 million).

Road Racing Increases in Popularity

Since the mid-1980s the popularity of road racing has more than doubled, to 7.1 million finishers in more than 12,000 U.S. running events during 1999, according to statistics of the USA Track and Field Road Running Information Center. With the increased participation has come a shift in the most popular distance for running. In the mid-1980s the most popular distance was 10 kilometers. Today, the most common distance is 5 kilometers. It has been estimated that 2.5 million persons finished a 5-kilometer race during 1999 and that 1 million finished a 10-kilometer race. An estimated 435,000 persons finished a marathon during 1999 and 445,000 finished a half-marathon.

Trail running has experienced an increase in popularity. American Sports Data (ASD) reported that 6.2 million Americans said they were trail runners during 1999, an increase of 181.7 percent over 1998. According to the ASD, the typical trail runner was 28.7 years old and had a household income of $63,000. Reflecting the general population of America's 34 million runners/joggers, estimates indicated that 56.6 percent of trail runners were male and 43.4 percent were female.

PETS—COMPANIONSHIP AND PLEASURE

Pets often provide more than recreation for their owners—they may become family members, and most people report that their pets bring pleasure to their lives. The American Animal Hospital Association (AAHA) reported in 1996 that 8 of 10 dog owners and three-fourths of cat owners bought their pets holiday or birthday presents. Some people, wanting to extend their pets' lives and improve their health, are willing to spend large amounts on veterinary care, some even buying health insurance for their pets. In a 1995 AAHA survey, when asked what companion they would choose if they were stranded on a desert island, 46 percent of respondents named a human companion, while 42 percent picked a dog, and 11 percent, a cat.

The numbers of dog owners and cat owners were almost equal. According to the Humane Society of the United States, there were about 62.4 million dog owners and 62.25 million cat owners during 1999. Four out of 10 households owned at least 1 dog, and 3 in 10 owned at least 1 cat.

Multiple-Pet Owners

Almost half of cat-owning households owned more than one cat. Cat owners in the south averaged 3.2 cats, as contrasted with cat owners in the northeast who averaged

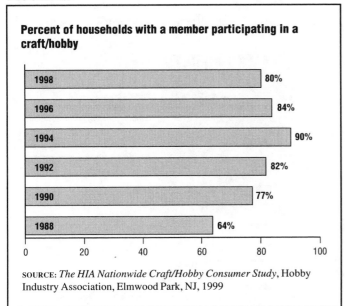

FIGURE 1.3

Percent of households with a member participating in a craft/hobby

Year	Percent
1998	80%
1996	84%
1994	90%
1992	82%
1990	77%
1988	64%

SOURCE: *The HIA Nationwide Craft/Hobby Consumer Study*, Hobby Industry Association, Elmwood Park, NJ, 1999

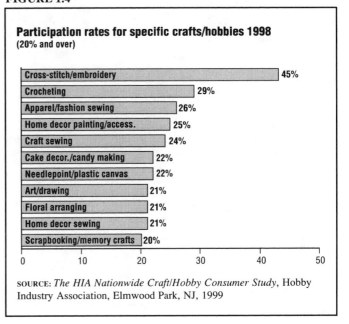

FIGURE 1.4

Participation rates for specific crafts/hobbies 1998
(20% and over)

Craft/Hobby	Percent
Cross-stitch/embroidery	45%
Crocheting	29%
Apparel/fashion sewing	26%
Home decor painting/access.	25%
Craft sewing	24%
Cake decor./candy making	22%
Needlepoint/plastic canvas	22%
Art/drawing	21%
Floral arranging	21%
Home decor sewing	21%
Scrapbooking/memory crafts	20%

SOURCE: *The HIA Nationwide Craft/Hobby Consumer Study*, Hobby Industry Association, Elmwood Park, NJ, 1999

1.8 cats. Households maintained more female cats (2.1 cats) than male cats (1.6 cats). One in 10 dog owners owned three or more dogs. Two in 10 owned two dogs. The gender of dog owners was distributed roughly equally between male and female.

Are Pets Substitutes for Children?

The Humane Society's figures indicated that households with no children under age 18 owned, on average, two dogs, as contrasted with other dog-owning households, which owned, on average, one dog. Households with one child owned more cats, on average (3.5 cats), than households with more than one child. Statistically, households with two children had fewer cats than households with one child, and households with three or more children had fewer cats than households with two children.

HOBBIES

A hobby is an activity that a person does for pleasure, not as one's primary business. Hobbies were once the mainstay of leisure time. While this sort of activity still exists, experts believe it is less popular, seeming to have been surpassed by collecting, a profit-motivated activity (see below). The U.S. Bureau of the Census reported that in 1980 there were 910 categories of hobby businesses in the United States, compared with 1,475 in 1990 and 1,548 in 1997. Because the population has grown by a far faster rate, however, this actually reflects a decline in the popularity of such businesses.

Some of the most common hobbies are cross-stitch/embroidery, crocheting, quilting, knitting, cake decorating, model-train collecting, wreath making, art/drawing, photography, gardening, studying genealogy, floral arrang-

ing, woodworking, and crossword puzzles. Teens often enjoy playing board games, drawing/painting and sculpting, playing musical instruments, and card collecting.

The Hobby Industry Association, an industry trade group, in *The HIA 1998 Nationwide Craft/Hobby Consumer Study* (1999), found that 80 percent of households reported that at least one member of the household engaged in a craft or hobby. That was down from 90 percent in 1994, but more than 1988's 64 percent. (See Figure 1.3.) The typical hobbyist spent an average of 7.5 hours per week on his or her hobby. Cross-stitch/embroidery was the most popular hobby (45 percent), followed by crocheting (29 percent), apparel/fashion sewing (26 percent), home decor painting (25 percent), and craft sewing (24 percent). (See Figure 1.4.) Hobbyists used their creations as gifts (71 percent), home decorating (69 percent), personal use (62 percent), holiday decorating (59 percent), and to sell (16 percent). (Some hobbyists used their hobbies for more than one use.)

Collecting as Recreation

Kalorama Information, in its *U.S. Giftware Market Place* (1998), found that collectibles represented the fastest-growing category of giftware sales in 1998 (see Chapter 2). Married, middle-aged women without children living at home were the prime market for collectibles—38 percent collected figurines; 27 percent, dolls; and 26 percent, plates. Christmas ornaments and teddy bears followed in popularity. Almost 44 percent collected for emotional or sentimental reasons, while 27 percent said they collected for decorating purposes and 10 percent for investment. Although substantially more women than men collected, men who collected were twice as likely as women to collect as an investment.

FIGURE 1.5

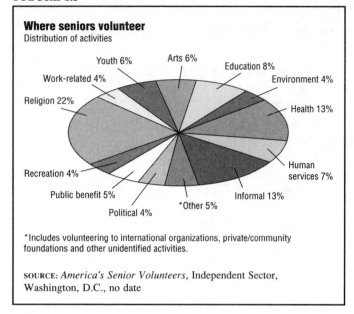

Where seniors volunteer
Distribution of activities

Youth 6% · Arts 6% · Education 8% · Environment 4%
Work-related 4% · Religion 22% · Health 13%
Recreation 4% · Human services 7%
Public benefit 5% · *Other 5% · Informal 13%
Political 4%

*Includes volunteering to international organizations, private/community foundations and other unidentified activities.

SOURCE: *America's Senior Volunteers*, Independent Sector, Washington, D.C., no date

FIGURE 1.6

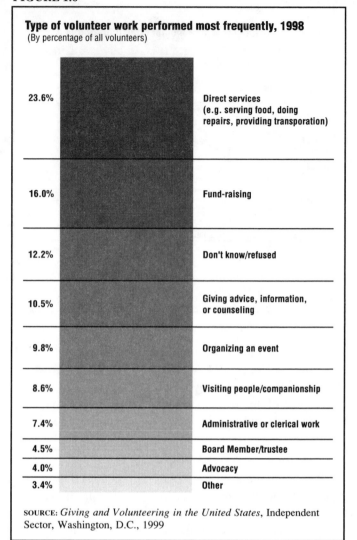

Type of volunteer work performed most frequently, 1998
(By percentage of all volunteers)

23.6%	Direct services (e.g. serving food, doing repairs, providing transporation)
16.0%	Fund-raising
12.2%	Don't know/refused
10.5%	Giving advice, information, or counseling
9.8%	Organizing an event
8.6%	Visiting people/companionship
7.4%	Administrative or clerical work
4.5%	Board Member/trustee
4.0%	Advocacy
3.4%	Other

SOURCE: *Giving and Volunteering in the United States*, Independent Sector, Washington, D.C., 1999

In 1997 adults collected 40 percent of action-figure toys, according to Unity Market's *Action Figures: Trend Report Profiling the Action Figure Market*. The action-figure market reached $2.1 billion in sales in 1997, up 27 percent from 1996. An estimated 10 million American households collected action figures, and the profile of the action-figure collector differed greatly from the traditional core collecting market. Action-figure collectors tended to be younger males, under 44 years of age, compared with the typical collector, a 45- to 64-year-old female. Action-figure collectors tended to be more ethnically diverse than collectors of other items, and they had overall lower household incomes than other collectors.

About 10 percent of U.S. households contained action-figure collections. This included households of both child and adult collectors. Science-fiction figures were the most popular in 1997, followed by comic-book superheroes, military figures, and musical entertainment and celebrity figures. Collectors valued increased size and details, more accessories and articulation, and the figures' ability to flex or move. (For a discussion of expenditures for collecting, see Chapter 2.)

VOLUNTEER WORK

Many Americans spend their leisure time in volunteer work helping others. Independent Sector (IS), in its 1999 national survey, found that an estimated 109 million people, or 56 percent of adults aged 18 and over, performed volunteer work during 1999. A total of 19.9 billion hours were given in volunteer service. Volunteering increased by 13.7 percent during 1999, to a level of volunteering participation that was the highest ever recorded by IS.

To give an idea of the magnitude of participation in volunteering, the volunteer workforce during 1999 repre-

sented the equivalent of more than 9 million full-time employees providing labor worth $225 billion.

Who Volunteers?

IS, in its *America's Senior Volunteers* (1998), found that almost 44 percent of seniors 55 and older volunteered at least once a year and that more than 36 percent had volunteered during the previous month. They contributed an average 4.4 hours per week, a total contribution to non-profit organizations of $70.5 billion worth of labor per year. Religious activities were volunteered for by 22 percent; informal activities, such as helping a neighbor, by 13 percent; health organizations, by 13 percent; and the remainder, for a variety of other activities. (See Figure 1.5.) Even after becoming elderly, seniors still volunteer. The IS 1999 survey found that 43 percent of seniors aged 75 and over reported volunteering.

More women (62 percent) than men (49 percent) volunteered during 1998, but men who volunteered gave slightly more time (3.6 hours) per week than did women (3.4 hours). There were increases in the numbers of Hispanics and African Americans who participated in volunteering during 1998. Hispanic volunteering participation increased by 6 percent and African American participation in volunteering increased by 12 percent, as compared with figures from 1995.

What Do Volunteers Do?

The IS survey found that the most popular volunteer activity (23.6 percent) involved providing direct service, such as serving food, making repairs, or providing transportation. (See Figure 1.6.) Fund-raising was another popular volunteer activity, with a participation rate of 16 percent. Other popular volunteer activities included giving advice or counseling (10.5 percent), organizing an event (9.8 percent), and visiting people or providing companionship (8.6 percent).

CHAPTER 2
THE COST OF HAVING FUN

CONSUMER EXPENDITURES FOR RECREATION

Americans are always finding new ways to spend their free time and money. In good economic times, people generally have more discretionary income to spend on leisure and recreation. The U.S. Bureau of Labor Statistics reported that in 1999 Americans spent an average of $1,891 on entertainment, barely more than the $1,834 that was spent in 1996. Persons aged 45–54 spent the most on recreation ($2,368), and those over 75, the least ($875). (See Table 2.1.)

In 1997 Americans spent a total of $462.9 billion on entertainment, up significantly from $370.2 billion in 1994. Most went toward lottery tickets; pet expenses; cable television; film processing; photographic studios; sporting and recreation camps; video rentals; and video, computer, and musical equipment. Toys and sports supplies accounted for $47.8 billion, and $48.1 billion was spent on personal transportation (including boats and pleasure aircraft), sports, and photographic equipment. (See Table 2.2.)

Trends during 1997 and 1998 had seen expenditures fall in the entertainment category. The average annual entertainment expenditure of $1,834 per person in 1996 fell to $1,813 in 1997 and $1,746 in 1998. (See Table 2.3.) This represented a drop of 1.1 percent from 1996 to 1997 and a 3.7 percent drop from 1997 to 1998. The average annual 1999 entertainment expenditure of $1,891, however, represented an increase of 8.3 percent over 1998.

Personal Recreation Expenditures

Data from the Bureau of Economic Analysis, a division of the U.S. Department of Commerce, showed that consumers steadily increased their total spending on entertainment events each year from 1993 through 1998. (See Table 2.4; note, in Tables 2.4 and 2.5, the term "nominal" means reported, and the term "real" means the figure

has been adjusted to account for inflation.) Americans spent $23.8 billion in 1998 to see performing arts, movies, and spectator sports.

In 1998 performing arts experienced the greatest increase from 1997 figures (8.05 percent), with total receipts of $9.4 billion. Spending on spectator sports increased 7.04 percent with total receipts of $7.6 billion. Movies brought in $6.8 billion at the box office, an increase of 6.25 percent over 1997. Between 1993 and 1998, "real" spending on performing arts and motion pictures each increased by 16 percent. Real spending on spectator sports increased by 14 percent during the same period.

The Computer Threat

Although total expenditures for entertainment increased between 1993 and 1998, Table 2.5 presents the data from a different perspective. Table 2.5 shows selected expenditures for types of recreation as a percentage of all recreation expenditures. In 1993 consumers spent 2.1 percent of their recreation dollars on performing arts events. By 1998 that figure had fallen to 1.68 percent.

The same pattern can be observed in other recreation areas. Consumers in 1993 spent 1.53 percent of their recreation dollars on movies. By 1998 the figure had dropped to 1.23 percent.

Expenditures on spectator sports, books, magazines, and gardening—all popular forms of entertainment for Americans—dropped as a percentage of total recreation dollars spent.

Where are these recreation dollars going? To computers. In 1993, 2.07 percent of recreation dollars were spent on computers, peripherals, and software. By 1998 that share had increased to a whopping 12.48 percent. Americans spent seven times as much on computers as on performing arts in 1998. The amount spent on computers, software, and peripherals during 1998 was twice as much

TABLE 2.1

Age of reference person: Average annual expenditures and characteristics, Consumer Expenditure Survey, 1999

Item	All consumer units	Under 25	25-34	35-44	45-54	55-64	65 and over	65-74	75 and over
Number of consumer units (in thousands)	108,465	8,164	19,332	24,405	20,903	13,647	22,015	11,578	10,437
Consumer unit characteristics:									
Income before taxes [1]	$43,951	$18,276	$42,470	$53,579	$59,822	$49,436	$26,581	$28,928	$23,937
Income after taxes [1]	40,363	17,431	39,405	49,616	54,459	42,809	25,325	27,567	22,800
Age of reference person	47.9	21.4	29.7	39.5	49.2	59.1	74.8	69.3	80.8
Average number in consumer unit:									
Persons	2.5	1.8	2.9	3.2	2.7	2.2	1.7	1.9	1.5
Children under 18	.7	.4	1.1	1.3	.6	.2	.1	.1	([2])
Persons 65 and over	.3	([2])	([2])	([2])	([2])	.1	1.4	1.4	1.3
Earners	1.3	1.3	1.5	1.7	1.8	1.3	.4	.6	.2
Vehicles	1.9	1.1	1.7	2.1	2.5	2.2	1.5	1.8	1.2
Percent distribution:									
Housing tenure:									
Homeowner	65	13	45	67	77	80	80	82	77
With mortgage	38	7	37	54	54	40	16	22	9
Without mortgage	27	6	8	13	22	40	64	60	68
Renter	35	87	55	33	23	20	20	18	23
Average annual expenditures	$37,027	$21,725	$36,181	$42,836	$46,538	$39,427	$26,553	$29,911	$22,900
Food	5,031	3,354	5,140	6,109	5,945	5,056	3,511	4,146	2,841
Food at home	2,915	1,828	2,890	3,537	3,340	2,920	2,266	2,575	1,943
Cereals and bakery products	448	271	432	561	509	433	357	399	314
Cereals and cereal products	160	102	170	211	175	140	116	130	101
Bakery products	288	169	262	350	335	294	242	269	213
Meats, poultry, fish, and eggs	749	469	751	897	878	761	563	664	457
Dairy products	322	195	322	410	354	305	255	289	220
Fruits and vegetables	500	283	475	572	563	525	450	497	401
Food away from home	2,116	1,526	2,250	2,572	2,605	2,136	1,245	1,571	898
Housing	12,057	6,585	12,520	14,215	14,513	12,093	8,946	9,605	8,230
Shelter	7,016	4,140	7,613	8,605	8,534	6,660	4,578	4,929	4,188
Owned dwellings	4,525	596	3,936	6,110	6,203	4,813	2,973	3,424	2,472
Mortgage interest and charges	2,547	311	2,694	3,990	3,642	2,328	745	1,038	420
Property taxes	1,123	168	751	1,297	1,444	1,380	1,149	1,222	1,069
Maintenance, repairs, insurance, other expenses	855	117	490	823	1,117	1,105	1,078	1,164	983
Rented dwellings	2,027	3,296	3,447	2,121	1,532	1,206	1,182	968	1,420
Other lodging	464	248	230	374	799	641	423	537	296
Utilities, fuels, and public services	2,377	1,166	2,249	2,587	2,819	2,608	2,145	2,369	1,897
Natural gas	270	92	238	283	304	327	284	290	276
Electricity	899	426	811	969	1,074	997	848	933	753
Fuel oil and other fuels	74	14	47	72	94	80	102	117	86
Telephone services	849	562	924	950	1,008	869	614	711	506
Water and other public services	285	72	229	313	339	335	298	319	276
Household operations	666	181	772	830	606	476	746	458	1,064
Personal services	323	121	573	500	148	60	311	87	559
Other household expenses	343	60	199	330	459	416	435	372	505
Apparel and services	1,743	1,192	2,047	2,053	2,048	1,722	1,070	1,235	901
Transportation	7,011	5,037	7,150	8,041	9,010	7,330	4,385	5,457	3,196
Vehicle purchases (net outlay)	3,305	2,859	3,500	3,807	4,117	3,406	1,911	2,422	1,344
Cars and trucks, new	1,628	857	1,377	1,722	2,079	2,109	1,304	1,661	907
Cars and trucks, used	1,641	1,974	2,034	2,058	1,988	1,283	606	758	437
Other vehicles	36	[3]28	89	27	51	[3]14	[3]2	[3]3	[4])
Gasoline and motor oil	1,055	708	1,066	1,259	1,349	1,093	644	807	463
Other vehicle expenses	$2,254	$1,253	$2,249	$2,565	$3,085	$2,339	$1,443	$1,724	$1,131
Public transportation	397	217	335	411	459	492	387	504	258
Health care	1,959	551	1,170	1,631	2,183	2,450	3,019	2,991	3,052
Entertainment	1,891	1,149	1,776	2,254	2,368	2,176	1,239	1,567	875
Personal care products and services	408	254	381	471	475	449	333	370	295
Reading	159	70	116	157	210	195	163	184	141
Education	635	1,277	453	637	1,125	552	139	165	111
Tobacco products and smoking supplies	300	220	295	370	395	329	148	204	86
Miscellaneous	889	370	745	984	1,104	1,041	807	803	812
Cash contributions	1,190	186	589	1,074	1,426	1,762	1,640	1,684	1,593
Personal insurance and pensions	3,436	1,110	3,433	4,455	5,415	3,941	980	1,280	647
Life and other personal insurance	394	61	238	418	616	533	333	429	226
Pensions and Social Security	3,042	1,049	3,195	4,037	4,799	3,408	647	851	421

[1] Components of income and taxes are derived from "complete income reporters" only.
[2] Value less than 0.05.
[3] Data are likely to have large sampling errors.
[4] No data reported.

SOURCE: *Consumer Expenditures in 1999*, U.S. Bureau of Labor Statistics, Washington, D.C., December 2000

as spent on books and maps; twice as much as spent on magazines, newspapers, and sheet music; 10 times as much as spent on movies; and 9 times as much as spent on spectator sports.

The Cost of a Night Out

A 1998 *Entertainment Marketing Letter* (EML) study found that it cost an average of $127.05 to take a family of four out for the night. EML also gathers data to find out average ticket costs to a movie, family show, rock/pop concert, classical concert, and live theater performance, as well as estimated spending at concession and merchandise stands for each type of entertainment.

The $127.05 represents an average ranging from $25.76 for a family to see a movie to $204.32 to attend a Broadway show or touring version of a stage production. The average cost of a rock/pop concert was $153.48. Among theme parks, it cost $93.80 per day for a family of four to visit Hershey Park (Pennsylvania), $143.80 for Busch Gardens (Florida), $152 for Sea World (Florida), $131.40 for Six Flags (New Jersey), and $646 for Walt Disney World (Florida).

CONSUMER ELECTRONICS

An explosion of technology has changed the consumer electronics industry. Digital technology has made possible a new array of products. The difference between information management and consumer electronics is beginning to blur. According to the Consumer Electronics Association (CEA), Americans spent $81 billion on consumer electronics in 1999, an increase of 6 percent over 1998. The average American household spent $1,000 per year on consumer electronic products.

America Goes Digital

According the CEA, digital products were the fastest-growing segment of the industry. In some cases, digital units already outsold analog models. Digital wireless phones offer mobile access to the Internet. Digital television provides dramatically better picture quality, new ways to store and manipulate information, and the possibility of interactivity. Digital audio provides new ways to deliver and store musical recordings. And the new technology permits consumer electronic devices to be made smaller and more portable.

Video

The CEA reported that video product sales surpassed 1998's figures by 22 percent in 1999, with 60 million units sold. Color TV sales were more than 23 million units. Americans purchased 125,000 high-definition televisions in 1999, but consumer electronics experts expected that many more than that would be sold in future years. Total videocassette recorder (VCR) sales increased 26

TABLE 2.2

Personal consumption expenditures for recreation: 1994–97

(Billions of dollars)

	1994	1995	1996	1997
Recreation	**370.2**	**404.2**	**432.3**	**462.9**
Books and maps (d.)	20.6	22.4	24.2	25.2
Magazines, newspapers, and sheet music (n.d.)	24.5	25.7	27.6	29.1
Nondurable toys and sport supplies (n.d.)	39.7	42.3	45.1	47.8
Wheel goods, sports and photographic equipment, boats, and pleasure aircraft (d.)	35.6	39.3	42.3	48.1
Video and audio products, computing equipment, and musical instruments (d.).	78.5	86.4	92.0	96.5
Radio and television repair (s.)	4.5	4.9	5.0	5.4
Flowers, seeds, and potted plants (n.d.)	13.4	13.8	14.8	15.9
Admissions to specified spectator amusements	19.0	20.1	21.9	23.3
Motion picture theaters (s.)	5.6	5.8	6.2	6.6
Legitimate theaters and opera, and entertainments of nonprofit institutions (except athletics) (s.).	8.2	8.7	9.3	10.0
Spectator sports [1] (s.)	5.2	5.5	6.4	6.7
Clubs and fraternal organizations [2] (s.)	11.8	12.7	13.0	13.8
Commercial participant amusements [3] (s.)	36.2	41.3	44.7	49.1
Pari-mutuel net receipts (s.)	3.3	3.3	3.4	3.5
Other [4] (s.)	83.1	92.1	98.3	105.1

[1] Consists of admissions to professional and amateur athletic events and to racetracks.
[2] Consists of dues and fees excluding insurance premiums.
[3] Consists of billiard parlors; bowling alleys; dancing, riding, shooting, skating, and swimming places; amusement devices and parks; golf courses; sightseeing buses and guides; private flying operations; casino gambling; and other commercial participant amusements.
[4] Consists of net receipts of lotteries and expenditures for purchases of pets and pet care services, cable TV, film processing, photographic studios, sporting and recreation camps, video cassette rentals, and recreational services, not elsewhere classified.
Note: Consumer durable goods are designated (d.), nondurable goods (n.d.), and services (s.).

SOURCE: *Survey of Current Business*, U.S. Bureau of Economic Analysis, August 1998

percent over 1998's numbers to 22 million. Sales of digital video disk (DVD) players increased from 1.1 million in 1998 to over 4 million in 1999. Also, compared with 1998's figures, direct-to-home satellite systems grew by 35 percent in 1999, with 3.6 million sales. At the beginning of the twenty-first century, about 10 percent of American homes had satellite TV.

Audio

The CEA reported that 45 million compact disc (CD) players were sold in 1999. Americans purchased 27 million portable headset audio products and 20 million radios. Overall, audio products experienced a 2.1 percent increase in sales in 1999.

Video Games

According to a study by NPD Group, a marketing information company, video game retail sales reached

TABLE 2.3

Annual expenditures of all consumer units and percent changes, 1996–98

Item	1996	1997	1998	Percent change 1996-97	1997-98
Number of consumer units (000's)	104,212	105,576	107,182		
Income before taxes[1]	$38,014	$39,926	$41,622		
Average age of reference person	47.7	47.7	47.6		
Average number in consumer unit:					
Persons	2.5	2.5	2.5		
Earners	1.3	1.3	1.3		
Vehicles	1.9	2.0	2.0		
Percent homeowner	64	64	64		
Average annual expenditures	$33,797	$34,819	$35,535	3.0	2.1
Food	4,698	4,801	4,810	2.2	.2
At home	2,876	2,880	2,780	.1	-3.5
Away from home	1,823	1,921	2,030	5.4	5.7
Housing	10,747	11,272	11,713	4.9	3.9
Apparel and services	1,752	1,729	1,674	-1.3	-3.2
Transportation	6,382	6,457	6,616	1.2	2.5
Health care	1,770	1,841	1,903	4.0	3.4
Entertainment	1,834	1,813	1,746	-1.1	-3.7
Personal insurance and pensions	3,060	3,223	3,381	5.3	4.9
Other expenditures	3,555	3,684	3,693	3.6	.2

[1] Income values are derived from "complete income reporters" only.

SOURCE: *Consumer Expenditures in 1998,* U.S. Bureau of Labor Statistics, Washington, D.C., November 1999

TABLE 2.4

Admission receipts for performing arts events, motion pictures, and spectator sports: 1993–98

	1998 $ billions		1997 $ billions		1996 $ billions		1995 $ billions		1994 $ billions		1993 $ Billions	
	Nominal	Real	Nominal	Real	Nominal	Real	Nominal	Real	Nominal	Real	Nominal	Real
Admission receipts to specified entertainments	$23.8	$22.6	$22.2	$21.6	$20.7	$20.7	$19.2	$20.2	$18.2	$19.8	$17.5	$19.7
(change from previous year)	7.21%	4.63%	7.25%	4.35%	7.81%	2.48%	5.49%	2.02%	4.00%	0.51%	8.70%	7.65%
Performing arts	$9.4	$8.9	$8.7	$8.4	$8.0	$8.0	$7.6	$8.0	$7.2	$7.8	$6.8	$7.7
(change from previous year)	8.05%	5.95%	8.75%	5.00%	5.26%	0.00%	5.56%	2.56%	5.88%	1.30%	13.33%	11.59%
Motion pictures	$6.8	$6.5	$6.4	$6.2	$5.8	$5.8	$5.5	$5.8	$5.2	$5.7	$5.0	$5.6
(change from previous year)	6.25%	4.84%	10.34%	6.90%	5.45%	0.00%	5.77%	1.75%	4.00%	1.79%	2.04%	0.00%
Spectator sports	$7.6	$7.2	$7.1	$6.9	$6.9	$6.9	$6.1	$6.4	$5.8	$6.3	$5.7	$6.3
(change from previous year)	7.04%	4.35%	2.90%	0.00%	13.11%	7.81%	5.17%	1.59%	1.75%	0.00%	11.76%	8.62%

Note: "Real" refers to estimates that are measured in 1996 chained dollars to control for inflation.

SOURCE: Research Division Note #75, National Endowment for the Arts, March 2000

$6.3 billion in 1998, an increase of 22 percent over 1997. Sales growth was expected to continue. In addition, because of technology developments, sales of all home entertainment devices, which include TV set-top boxes, handheld computers, and gaming consoles, were expected to increase dramatically. International Data Corporation, a research organization, predicted sales of home entertainment devices would increase from 11 million sold in 1999 to 89 million by 2004.

SPORTING GOODS SALES

Sports Apparel

Americans have become very aware of their personal health and fitness. Some Americans who take part in physical fitness activities, such as jogging or walking, or who play active sports, such as softball or skiing, often feel they must dress as if they were professional players. According to the Sporting Goods Manufacturers Associa-

TABLE 2.5

GDP, consumption expenditures, and recreation expenditures

	1998	1997	1996	1995	1994	1993
Real GDP	$8,516	$8,165	$7,813	$7,537	$7,338	$7,054
(change from previous year)	4.30%	4.50%	3.66%	2.72%	4.02%	2.37%
Real personal consumption expenditures	$5,699	$5,434	$5,238	$5,070	$4,920	$4,742
(change from previous year)	4.88%	3.75%	3.30%	3.05%	3.76%	3.00%
Real recreation expenditures	$512	$465	$430	$399	$365	$338
(change from previous year)	10.25%	8.15%	7.75%	9.17%	7.95%	8.08%
Selected expenditures as a % of all real recreation expenditures	**1998**	**1997**	**1996**	**1995**	**1994**	**1993**
Admissions to performing arts events	1.68%	1.72%	1.84%	1.97%	2.04%	2.10%
Admissions to motion picture theaters	1.23%	1.27%	1.33%	1.43%	1.49%	1.53%
Admissions to spectator sports	1.36%	1.41%	1.59%	1.57%	1.65%	1.72%
Books and maps	5.23%	5.66%	5.80%	5.99%	6.02%	6.00%
Magazines, newspapers, and sheet music	6.03%	6.28%	6.42%	6.82%	7.34%	7.60%
Flowers, seeds, and potted plants	3.28%	3.47%	3.47%	3.36%	3.61%	3.69%
Computers, peripherals, and software	12.48%	8.20%	5.49%	3.66%	2.74%	2.07%

Note: "Real" refers to estimates that are measured in 1996 chained dollars to control for inflation.

SOURCE: Research Division Note #75, National Endowment for the Arts, March 2000

tion (SGMA), manufacturers' sales of all sports apparel totaled $38.8 billion in 1998, increasing by almost twice as much as the increase in sales revenue for apparel of all kinds. The SGMA noted that "active" sports apparel sales did not grow much, but "total" sports apparel sales did. This indicated that a major part of sports apparel purchases were not for active participation in sport, but were for fashion or comfort.

According to a 1997 SGMA study, only 20 percent of sports apparel purchased was bought with the intention of using it to play sports. More than half of sports apparel consumers used their clothing for multiple purposes: exercise and sports, recreational activities, and everyday use. Only 15 percent of men and 7 percent of women cited competition as the primary reason for buying sports apparel. Sports apparel was worn to work by 57 percent of buyers. Almost 30 percent of buyers reported they wore sports apparel to work on "casual Fridays."

Sales for men's sports apparel increased almost twice as fast as sales for women's sports apparel, but the total dollar value of each was about equal in 1998. Women made most of the sports apparel purchases (81.1 percent), whether the sports apparel products were for men, women, or children.

Sports apparel did see a 2.7 percent sales increase in 1999, with total sales of $20 billion wholesale, the largest revenue segment of the sporting goods industry. Sales of sport shirts led the way at $6.6 billion.

Almost 44 percent of sports apparel is worn by persons less than 20 years of age. Another major segment of the market is persons aged 45 and older, who wear about 24 percent of the apparel. Experts predicted that as baby

FIGURE 2.1

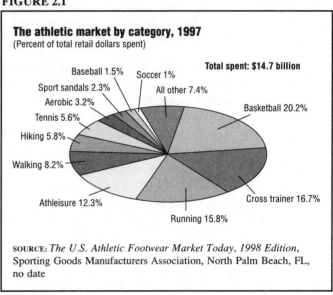

The athletic market by category, 1997
(Percent of total retail dollars spent)

Total spent: $14.7 billion

- Baseball 1.5%
- Soccer 1%
- Sport sandals 2.3%
- All other 7.4%
- Aerobic 3.2%
- Tennis 5.6%
- Hiking 5.8%
- Walking 8.2%
- Athleisure 12.3%
- Running 15.8%
- Cross trainer 16.7%
- Basketball 20.2%

SOURCE: *The U.S. Athletic Footwear Market Today, 1998 Edition,* Sporting Goods Manufacturers Association, North Palm Beach, FL, no date

boomers get into their fifties, there will be an upsurge in sports apparel sales to the "mature" market.

Athletic Footwear

Sales of athletic footwear reached $14.7 billion in 1997. Basketball shoes were the largest footwear category. Basketball (20 percent), cross-training (17 percent), and running shoes (16 percent) accounted for more than half of the sports footwear market. (See Figure 2.1.) Only 20 percent of all pairs of athletic shoes were intended primarily for use in sports or exercise.

In 1999, $13.74 billion was spent at the retail level on athletic footwear, a decline from 1997 levels. Data from the SGMA report found that consumers purchased 313.1

FIGURE 2.2

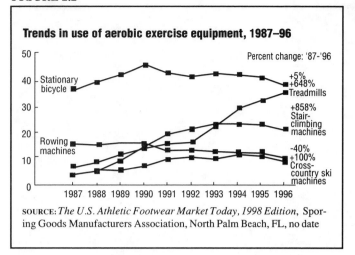

Trends in use of aerobic exercise equipment, 1987–96

SOURCE: *The U.S. Athletic Footwear Market Today, 1998 Edition*, Sporting Goods Manufacturers Association, North Palm Beach, FL, no date

TABLE 2.6

Travel expenditures in the U.S.
(Billions of dollars)

	Domestic	International
1986	$216	$26
1987	235	31
1988	258	38
1989	273	47
1990	291	58
1991	296	54
1992	308	71
1993	322	75
1994	339	78
1995	360	80
1996	383	90
1997	408	94

SOURCE: Travel Industry Association of America, Washington, D.C., 1999

million pairs of athletic shoes in 1999. The average price paid per pair was $43.89. Consumers aged 25–34 spent the most money on athletic footwear. Consumers confirmed, as they had in 1997, that most of them bought athletic shoes for casual wear rather than for any other purpose. Comfort was cited as the most important characteristic when selecting an athletic shoe.

Wholesale sales of athletic footwear reveal that running/jogging shoes were the most popular type of athletic shoe in 1999 ($1.68 billion). Other popular types of athletic shoes were cross-training ($1.39 billion), basketball ($1.29 billion), and athleisure ($1.11 billion). Though there was an overall decline in athletic shoe sales in 1999, the SGMA reported that sales of sports sandals and running/jogging shoes were up in 1999: 25 percent and 11.3 percent, respectively, over 1998.

Sports Equipment

The SGMA reported that sports equipment sales grew by 1.5 percent in 1999. The largest amount of wholesale revenue came from exercise equipment and machines ($3.47 billion). Golf equipment and firearms/hunting each had more than $2 billion in sales. Camping gear sold $1.66 billion retail. Fishing was the only category that experienced a significant increase in sales during 1999 (5 percent), with about $1 billion in wholesale sales.

In team sports, the three largest categories of sales during 1999 were baseball/softball ($424 million), basketball ($340 million), and soccer ($210 million).

Exercise Equipment

The SGMA found that, in 1997, adults in half of all American households owned at least one piece of exercise equipment, and it was used regularly in two out of three of those households. Exercise equipment was owned in 49.8 million homes (50.1 percent of the U.S. total of 99.3 mil-

lion). The Fitness Products Council estimated that consumers spent $4.8 billion for home exercise equipment.

Owners of fitness equipment were about equally male and female. Those 25–34 owned 24 percent of the equipment; 35–44, 23 percent; 55 and over, 22 percent; 45–54, 18 percent; and 18–24, 13 percent. The most frequently owned equipment was free weights, followed by treadmills and stationary bikes. The average amount spent for any single piece of equipment was $392. Figure 2.2 shows the trends in the use of aerobic exercise machines (stationary bicycles, rowing machines, cross-country skiing machines, stair climbers, and treadmills) from 1987 to 1996. Since 1996 sales of fitness equipment slowed but remained stronger than other segments of the sporting goods industry. The SGMA estimated that wholesale sales of fitness equipment rose 6 percent in 1999, to $3.57 billion.

A major reason for the surge in fitness-related activities comes from the growing number of older Americans who want to stay healthy and "young." That trend is expected to continue as a growing emphasis on lifetime fitness drives the market.

Recreational Transport Expenses

Recreational transport sales, which include bicycles, pleasure boats/motors, recreational vehicles, and snowmobiles, grew by 12.9 percent in 1999 to $17.38 billion. The growth was attributed partly to strong sales of recreational vehicles, which increased from $6.27 billion in 1998 to $7.09 billion in 1999. Another contributor to the increase was sales for pleasure boats and motors, which grew from $6.56 billion in 1998 to $7.75 billion in 1999.

The National Marine Manufacturers Association (NMMA) estimated that, in 1998, 74.8 million Americans

TABLE 2.7

Forecast for the U.S. travel and tourism industry

	1996	1997	1998	1999	2000	2001
Total U.AS. person-trips (millions)	994.2	1,026.6	1,064.9	1,081.8	1,097.1	1,116.3
Percent change	-0.1%	3.3%	3.7%	1.6%	1.4%	1.7%
Total international vistors (millions)	46.5	47.8	48.8	50.4	52.2	54.1
Percent change	7.3%	2.8%	2.3%	3.2%	3.5%	3.8%
Travel price inflation	168.1	173.7	178.2	185.4	192	198.1
Percent change	3.7%	3.4%	2.6%	4.1%	3.5%	3.2%
Travel expenditures (billions)						
U.S. residents	$382.6	$408.2	$434.4	$459.1	$482.1	$506.2
Percent change	6.1%	6.7%	6.4%	5.7%	5.0%	5.0%
International visitors*	$69.8	$73.3	$81.1	$87.5	$94.3	$101.5
Percent change	10.0%	5.0%	10.7%	7.9%	7.8%	7.6%
Total travel expenditures (billions)	**$452.4**	**$481.5**	**$515.5**	**$546.6**	**$576.4**	**$607.7**
Percent change	**6.7%**	**6.4%**	**7.1%**	**6.0%**	**5.5%**	**5.4%**

Note: * includes spending within the U.S. only.

SOURCE: Travel Industry Association of America, Washington, D.C., 1999

participated in recreational boating. Americans owned about 1.6 million sailboats and approximately 2.4 million miscellaneous craft, such as canoes and rowboats. There were 10,320 marinas, boatyards, yacht clubs, dockominiums, and parks in the United States in 1998. The NMMA estimated that Americans spent more than $19.1 billion on retail expenditures for boating in 1998, up from $13.7 billion in 1990.

TRAVEL COSTS

Travel and tourism is the United States's largest services export industry. It also is the third-largest retail sales category and one of America's largest employers. An estimated 12 percent of U.S. residents work in the tour industry, resulting in a $127.8 billion in payroll in 1997. An additional 9.2 million jobs received indirect support.

The travel industry is one of the nation's fastest-growing industries. In 1997, according to the Travel Industry Association of America (TIA), domestic and international travelers spent $1.38 billion a day. Expenditures for domestic travel totaled $408 billion in 1997, up from $235 billion in 1987. International travelers spent $94 billion in 1997. (See Table 2.6.) This spending generated more than $70 billion in tax revenues for federal, state, and local governments.

The TIA found that travel sales on the Internet reached $911 million in 1997, with 84 percent of online transactions being airline tickets. The American Car Rental Association reported that 55 million people rented cars that year. The average rental was 4.7 days, and the average price per rental was $158.11.

The TIA predicted that tourism would continue to grow. By 2001 person trips were expected to exceed 1.12 billion, up from 1.03 billion in 1997. Fifty-four million people were expected to travel internationally, up from 48 million in 1997. Total travel expenses were expected to increase from $482 billion in 1997 to $608 billion in 2001. (See Table 2.7.)

Many Americans pay for their vacations with their federal tax refunds. Nearly one-third (31 percent, 62 million) of American adults said they would include a vacation as part of their tax refund spending plans. Of those vacationers, 16 percent would take a vacation only if they received a tax refund. Americans most likely to use their tax refunds for vacation were between 18 and 24 years of age, were in households with incomes less than $30,000 annually, and had children in the home.

AMUSEMENT PARK EXPENDITURES

Americans have always enjoyed amusement parks and attractions such as Busch Gardens, Disneyland, and Six Flags. Big amusement parks and theme parks featuring children's rides, roller coasters, and water slides have

FIGURE 2.3

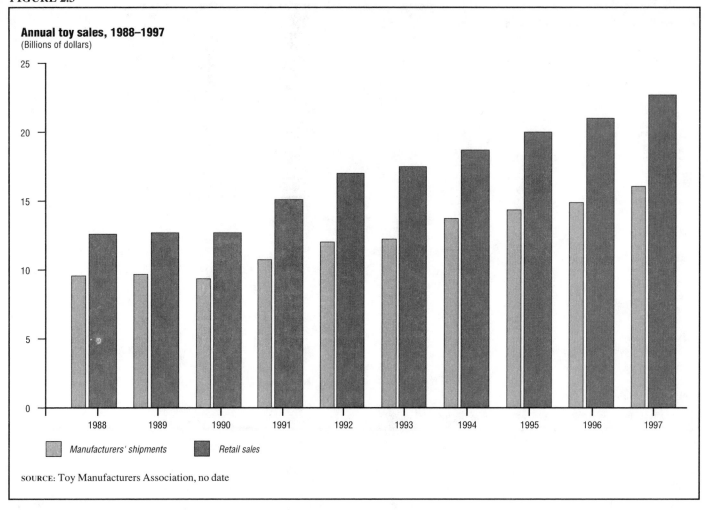

Annual toy sales, 1988–1997
(Billions of dollars)

Manufacturers' shipments   Retail sales

SOURCE: Toy Manufacturers Association, no date

existed in the United States since the early years of the twentieth century. In 1996 the amusement park industry had receipts of $6.8 billion, up from $4.9 billion in 1990.

SPENDING ON TOYS

Buying and playing with toys is a popular activity in the United States. In the past, the toy industry considered children 0–14 as their prime audience. Today, the prime toy-purchasing years are 0–10 years of age. The grandparent/older-adult market accounts for 14 percent of toy purchases. The TMA estimated that $350 was spent per child annually. In 1997 U.S. toy imports totaled $12.7 billion, primarily from China, Japan, and Mexico; the United States exported approximately $1.3 billion worth of toys to foreign nations.

The United States is the largest market for toys in the world, followed by Western Europe, Asia, and Japan. U.S. toy sales in 1997 rose to $23 billion, up from $13 billion in 1988. (See Figure 2.3.) While some toys may sell very well one year and then disappear the next year, other toys sell very well year-to-year. These steady bestsellers are the basis of the toy business and include

games, such as Monopoly and Chutes and Ladders, and preschool and infant toys, such as trains and plush animals. In 1997 the leader in (wholesale) toy sales was video games ($4.3 billion), followed by miscellaneous toys ($3.2 billion), dolls ($2.1 billion), activity toys ($2.1 billion), games/puzzles ($1.8 billion), vehicles ($1.5 billion), infant/preschool toys ($1.4 billion), stuffed toys ($1.4 billion), and action figures ($1.1 billion). (See Table 2.8.)

SPENDING ON BOOKS

Sales of all books climbed steadily in the late 1990s. The Book Industry Study Group found that sales of all books, excluding standard texts, reached an estimated $22.3 billion in 1998. (See Table 2.9.) Most books sold (860 million) and most revenue ($6.1 billion) came from the trade category. The study from which the data came, *Book Industry Trends 1999,* predicted that book sales would increase to $38.1 billion by 2003. Estimates for sales of books of all types for 1998, 1999, and 2000, respectively, were $28.7 billion, $30.5 billion, and $32.2 billion. Sales of children's books were expected to grow by 10.2 percent in 2000 to $1.9 billion.

TABLE 2.8

Wholesale toy sales in 1997

(Billions of dollars)

Action figure toys	$1.055
Activity toys	$2.078
Dolls	$2.113
Games/puzzles	$1.765
Infant/preschool toys	$1.378
Miscellaneous toys	$3.224
Ride-ons (excl. bikes)	$ .748
Stuffed toys	$1.353
Vehicles	$1.526
Video games	$4.276

SOURCE: Toy Manufacturers Association, no date

TABLE 2.9

Publishers' net dollar sales, 1998

(Billions of dollars)

Category	Estimates:
Trade	6.15
Mass market rack-size	1.51
Book clubs	1.21
Mail order publications	.47
Religious	1.18
Professional	4.42
University press	.39
Elhi	3.32
College	2.89
Subscription reference	.77
All books (excl. std. tests)	22.30

SOURCE: *Book Industry Trends 1999*, Book Industry Study Group, New York, New York, no date

Large chain bookstores sell the greatest volume of books to adult shoppers every year, about one and a half times as many as small chain bookstores and independent bookstores sell. There was strong growth, however, in sales in bookselling outlets in discount stores. Although they sold only about half as many volumes as small chain bookstores and independent bookstores in 1996, their growth in sales increased 22 percent between 1995 and 1996.

Total books sold increased from 1.037 billion in 1998 to 1.071 billion in 1999, according to estimates of the American Booksellers Association (ABA). America is changing, however, the way it buys books. The ABA's study reported that the adult market share continued to shift from traditional chain and independent bookstores in favor of Internet and mass-merchandisers. The ABA noted that the e-commerce/Internet category saw an increase in market share from 2 percent in 1998 to 5 percent in 1999.

Another ABA study revealed that, by late 1999, over 22 million adults were shopping for books online. Those who purchased books online said they purchased about half of their books that way. Almost 80 percent of online book purchasers ordered more than one book during the year, and nearly 40 percent ordered five or more books online. Clearly, book purchasing over the Internet has a rosy future.

COSTS OF WILDLIFE-RELATED RECREATION

Many Americans enjoy participating in recreation that involves wildlife. Fishing and hunting remain among the most popular forms of recreation in the United States, and increasing numbers of people enjoy watching, photographing, and feeding wild animals and birds. (For a discussion of wildlife-associated recreation, see Chapter 3.)

The U.S. Department of the Interior's *1996 National Survey of Fishing, Hunting, and Wildlife-Associated Recreation* (1997) found that, in 1996, Americans spent

FIGURE 2.4

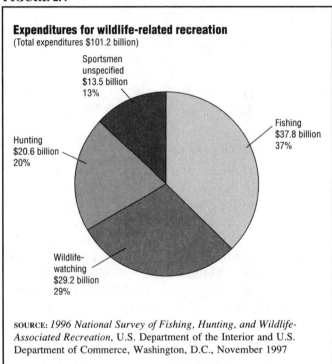

Expenditures for wildlife-related recreation
(Total expenditures $101.2 billion)

Sportsmen unspecified $13.5 billion 13%

Fishing $37.8 billion 37%

Hunting $20.6 billion 20%

Wildlife-watching $29.2 billion 29%

SOURCE: *1996 National Survey of Fishing, Hunting, and Wildlife-Associated Recreation*, U.S. Department of the Interior and U.S. Department of Commerce, Washington, D.C., November 1997

an estimated $101.2 billion on wildlife-related recreation. Fishing accounted for approximately 38 percent of that expense; wildlife-watching activities, 29 percent; and hunting, 21 percent. (Another 13 percent was unspecific.) (See Figure 2.4.) Of the expenditure by sportsmen, 61 percent was for equipment, 29 percent was trip-related, and 11 percent was "other." (See Figure 2.5.)

Americans who enjoyed watching wildlife spent an estimated $29.2 billion in 1996. Of that amount, 57 percent was for equipment; 32 percent was trip-related; and 11 percent was other (such as magazines, membership dues, and contributions to conservation or wildlife-related organizations). (See Figure 2.6.) Although the number of participants

FIGURE 2.5

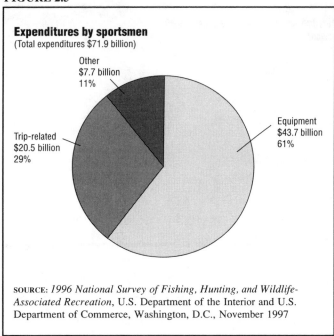

Expenditures by sportsmen
(Total expenditures $71.9 billion)

Other
$7.7 billion
11%

Trip-related
$20.5 billion
29%

Equipment
$43.7 billion
61%

SOURCE: *1996 National Survey of Fishing, Hunting, and Wildlife-Associated Recreation,* U.S. Department of the Interior and U.S. Department of Commerce, Washington, D.C., November 1997

FIGURE 2.6

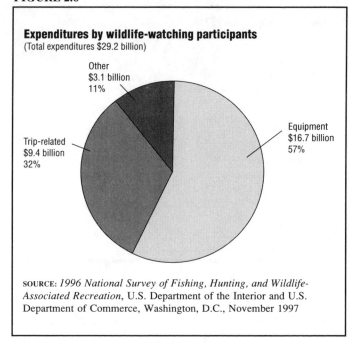

Expenditures by wildlife-watching participants
(Total expenditures $29.2 billion)

Other
$3.1 billion
11%

Trip-related
$9.4 billion
32%

Equipment
$16.7 billion
57%

SOURCE: *1996 National Survey of Fishing, Hunting, and Wildlife-Associated Recreation,* U.S. Department of the Interior and U.S. Department of Commerce, Washington, D.C., November 1997

has declined somewhat, those who do participate spend more—on more expensive equipment—than previously.

BUYING COLLECTIBLES

The U.S. Giftware Market, prepared by Kalorama Information, tracks purchases of giftware, which include collectibles, novelties, decorative accessories, and seasonal decorative accessories. In its 1998 study, the report found that annual sales of giftware reached almost $21 million. Collectibles, the most dynamic category, accounting for $5.45 billion of the $20.86 billion giftware market, grew at an annual rate of 11.2 percent and represented 26 percent of total giftware sales. The study noted a growing "cocooning trend," as the importance of the home as a place of leisure, entertainment, and work continued to grow. The concept of family collecting has grown as baby boomers find collecting a way to spend time with their children.

Giftware and collectible purchasers tended to be middle- to working-class high school graduates, with household incomes under $30,000. Those aged 18–34 spent about $21 per purchase, while those over age 55 spent just $15. The largest number of purchasers (36 percent) spent less than $30 on the last gift they purchased; 28 percent spent $30–49; and 30 percent spent $50 or more. (For a discussion of collecting as a hobby, see Chapter 1.)

SPENDING ON HOBBIES

The Hobby Industry Association, a professional organization for the hobby and craft industry, reported, in its *1996/97 Size of Craft/Hobby Industry Study,* that con-

sumer spending jumped from $7.8 billion in 1994 to $10.9 billion in 1996, a 37 percent increase. In 1997 consumers spent an estimated 35 percent of sales on general crafts; 31 percent on sewing crafts; 13 percent on needlecrafts; 11 percent on floral crafts; and 10 percent of the total on painting and drawing. (See Figure 2.7.) (For a discussion of participation in hobbies, see Chapter 1.)

PAYING TO TAKE A RISK

Weekend daredevils may encounter a variety of insurance problems, depending on the pastime and the danger involved. People who participate in high-risk recreational pursuits may find themselves forced to pay high rates for insurance coverage or be unable to get such coverage at all. When approached by people who participate in risky activities, insurance companies may decline to insure them, exclude accidents related to the dangerous activity, postpone coverage until after a specific event, or require a physical examination to renew such a policy. In some cases, they may find the activity not so serious and sell the policy at no additional cost.

Some insurance companies have added questions pertaining to risk behaviors. Various sports can add hundreds or thousands of dollars in annual premiums. Hobbies that involve great speed—auto, motorcycle, and boat racing—tend to make insurers most nervous. Disability insurers are more likely to reject such an applicant than other types of carriers. Disability claims have increased drastically, with some insurers losing money and leaving the business.

Sports associations sometimes step in to provide insurance when other carriers will not. The Professional

FIGURE 2.7

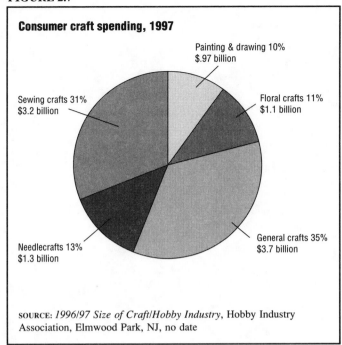

Consumer craft spending, 1997

Painting & drawing 10%
$.97 billion

Floral crafts 11%
$1.1 billion

Sewing crafts 31%
$3.2 billion

General crafts 35%
$3.7 billion

Needlecrafts 13%
$1.3 billion

SOURCE: *1996/97 Size of Craft/Hobby Industry*, Hobby Industry
Association, Elmwood Park, NJ, no date

Association of Diving Instructors offers certified scuba
divers medical insurance. The U.S. Hang Gliding Association has a $1 million liability policy to cover a glider
who sails into bystanders. The American Motorcyclist
Association sells its racers some medical coverage and
accidental death and dismemberment insurance.

CHAPTER 3
OUTDOOR RECREATION

THE LURE OF THE OUTDOORS

Americans love the outdoors. Millions of Americans spend their free time participating in outdoor activities. Surveys by the Sporting Goods Manufacturers Association (SGMA) found that recreational swimming was the most popular outdoor activity, with 95 million participants during 1999. (See Table 3.1.) Recreational bicycling was the second-most popular activity, with 56 million participants. Other popular outdoor activities included freshwater fishing (44 million), tent camping (41 million), and day hiking (39 million).

Not only do many Americans participate in recreational swimming and bicycling, they do so with great frequency. Bicyclists, in particular, were most likely to say they biked frequently. Of the 56 million people who participated in bicycling during 1999, 17 million of them said they biked frequently. (See Table 3.2.)

Roper Starch Worldwide, in *Outdoor Recreation in America (1999): The Family and the Environment,* an annual national survey of recreation patterns, reported increasing rates of participation. (See Figure 3.1 and Table 3.3.) For example, the study showed that the number of people who participated in outdoor recreation several times a week increased from 20 percent in 1998 to 24 percent in 1999. There also were increases in the percentage of Americans who participated in outdoor recreation one or more times per month. Similarly, the number of Americans who did not participate in outdoor activities at least once a year dropped from 29 percent to 20 percent.

America's love of the outdoors is increasing. A 1999 SGMA survey found that 4 of the 5 most popular sports were outdoor activities (recreational swimming, walking, bicycling, and freshwater fishing). Indeed, if tent camping and day hiking are considered, then 7 of the top 10 sports during 1999 were outdoor activities. The SGMA also found that persons who engaged in frequent sport or recreational activity were most likely to engage in outdoor activity. During 1999, 64.7 million Americans engaged in frequent activity. Not only was this the most in any category of activity, it was second only to strength training in terms of increase over 1998 figures.

TABLE 3.1

America's most popular outdoor activities in 1999
(6 years of age or older; in thousands; participated at least once)

Activity	Participation
1. Recreational swimming	95,094
2. Recreational bicycling	56,227
3. Freshwater fishing	44,452
4. Tent camping	40,803
5. Day hiking	39,235
6. Recreational vehicle camping	17,577
7. Horseback riding	16,906
8. Hunting (shotgun/rifle)	16,779
9. Saltwater fishing	14,807
10. Target shooting (rifle)	14,172

SOURCE: Sporting Goods Manufacturers Association, North Palm Beach, FL, August 28, 1998

TABLE 3.2

"Frequent" participation in America's outdoor activities in 1999
(6 years of age or older; in thousands)

Activity	"Frequent" participation
1. Recreational bicycling	17,151 (52+)*
2. Recreational swimming	16,743 (52+)
3. Freshwater fishing	13,176 (15+)
4. Day hiking	7,872 (15+)
5. Recreational vehicle camping	5,920 (15+)
6. Hunting (shotgun/rifle)	5,665 (15+)
7. Tent camping	4,838 (15+)
8. Saltwater fishing	3,501 (15+)
9. Target shooting (rifle)	3,475 (15+)
10. Target shooting (pistol)	2,804 (15+)

* ( ) days per year

SOURCE: Sporting Goods Manufacturers Association, North Palm Beach, FL, August 28, 1998

FIGURE 3.1

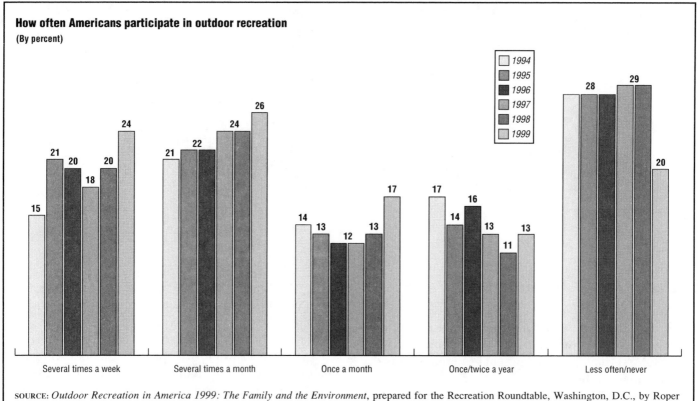

How often Americans participate in outdoor recreation
(By percent)

Legend: 1994, 1995, 1996, 1997, 1998, 1999

Several times a week: 15, 21, 20, 18, 20, 24
Several times a month: 21, 22, 24, 24, 26
Once a month: 14, 13, 12, 13, 17
Once/twice a year: 17, 14, 16, 13, 11, 13
Less often/never: 28, 28, 28, 29, 29, 20

SOURCE: *Outdoor Recreation in America 1999: The Family and the Environment*, prepared for the Recreation Roundtable, Washington, D.C., by Roper Starch, 1999

WHO ENGAGES IN OUTDOOR ACTIVITY, AND WHY

A Family Affair

Recreation often starts with the family. Many Americans began the recreational activities they enjoy as adults while still children. A 1998 survey prepared by Roper for the Recreation Roundtable found that parents who emphasized and participated in outdoor activities raised children who were more likely to become participants in, and supporters of, outdoor activities. Of parents with children at home, 42 percent reported that their children participated in outdoor recreation about the same amount as they did at the same age.

The survey also revealed a decline in the number of Americans reporting that outdoor recreation was important as a family activity. In 1986, 32 percent said recreation was important when they were growing up, and 48 percent said somewhat important. By 1998, only 23 percent reported it was very important, and 34 percent said it was somewhat important. Since young people reported, in general, similar participation rates as their parents, the study suggested that young people's participation today is more on their own or with friends rather than family.

The 1999 Roper study found that 45 percent of all Americans said they engaged in outdoor recreation as a family at least once a month. Of those who said they never engaged in outdoor recreation, about two-fifths were over 60 years of age and likely did not have children living with them.

Households with children 7 years of age or younger were most likely to recreate outdoors as a family at least once a month. Of such households, 65 percent said they did so, compared with 59 percent of households with children aged 8–17.

Why do Americans think children should engage in outdoor recreation? When asked why today's young people should engage in outdoor activities, the following reasons were the top ones given: promotes good health (72 percent), creates shared experiences family and friends can bond over (70 percent), teaches appreciation of nature (69 percent), helps children develop important physical skills (68 percent), builds self-esteem and personal growth (65 percent), and helps children develop important interpersonal skills (62 percent).

Kids Like the Outdoors

The *1998 Roper Youth Report* found that, among children aged 6–17, 53 percent preferred sports and outdoor activities in their free time. Only "hanging out"/playing with friends (59 percent) was enjoyed by more young people.

An SGMA study listed the top 10 activities in which children aged 6–17 participated frequently during 1999. The study found bicycling to be first and recreational

TABLE 3.3

Outdoor recreation participation during past year
(Percent who have participated in during past year)

	1994 %	1995 %	1996 %	1997 %	1998 %	1999 %	Pt. change since 1998 %
Walking for fitness/recreation	NA	45	39	42	47	42	-5
Driving for pleasure	40	36	33	34	39	35	-4
Swimming	35	31	28	31	33	40	+7
Picnicking	33	29	24	26	30	32	+2
Fishing	26	24	22	20	22	28	+6
Bicycling	21	20	16	19	19	22	+3
Visiting cultural sites	NA	NA	12	14	18	16	-2
Hiking	18	18	12	15	17	15	-2
Wildlife viewing	18	15	10	14	16	15	-1
Running/jogging	19	16	13	12	16	16	—
Outdoor photography	15	15	10	13	15	12	-3
Campground camping	16	16	12	12	15	21	+6
Golf	11	12	11	11	12	12	—
Bird watching	14	11	8	11	10	11	+1
Back packing	13	12	8	7	10	10	—
Motorboating	10	9	5	8	9	11	+2
RV camping	8	8	6	7	7	9	+2
Hunting	8	7	7	5	7	8	+1
Off road vehicle driving	5	5	5	5	7	7	—
In-line skating	NA	4	4	5	6	5	-1
Tennis	9	9	7	8	5	6	+1
Downhill skiing	6	6	5	5	5	4	-1
Canoeing/kayaking	6	5	4	5	5	7	+2
Target shooting	8	6	5	4	5	7	+2
Personal water craft (e.g. jet skis)	NA	NA	NA	3	5	5	—
Motorcycling	7	5	6	4	4	6	+2
Horseback riding	6	5	5	4	4	6	+2
Mountain biking	5	5	4	4	4	6	+2
Waterskiing	6	6	3	4	4	6	+2
Rock climbing	4	4	3	3	4	3	-1
Sailing	4	3	3	3	2	3	+1
Snorkeling/scuba diving	4	3	3	3	3	4	+1
Cross-country skiing	2	3	2	2	2	1	-1
Snowmobiling	2	3	2	1	2	2	—
Rowing	3	2	1	2	1	1	—
Snowboarding	NA	NA	NA	NA	1	3	+2

(NA) denotes not asked

SOURCE: *Outdoor Recreation in America 1999: The Family and the Environment,* prepared for the Recreation Roundtable, Washington, D.C., by Roper Starch, 1999

swimming and in-line skating to be third and fourth, respectively. Basketball was second. (See Chapter 5 for a discussion of team sports such as basketball.)

Middle America Likes the Outdoors

The 1999 Roper study found interesting demographic patterns among participants in outdoor activities. For example, frequency of outdoor activity increased with income. Americans in more affluent households were more likely to engage in outdoor activities at least once a month. The greatest increase in participation between 1998 and 1999, however, occurred among Americans in households with incomes between $15,000 and $29,999. Participation rates increased 18 percent for this group.

The study also found that persons aged 18–29 and persons who were PC users were more likely than the general public to engage in outdoor activities at least once a month. (See Figure 3.2.) Of persons in those two categories, 77 percent engaged in outdoor activity at least monthly, compared with 67 percent of the general public.

Outdoor activity was engaged in at least monthly by 78 percent of persons in households exceeding $50,000 per year in annual income, and by 85 percent of persons in households exceeding $70,000 in annual income. Persons in the Midwest were most likely to engage in outdoor activity: 81 percent did so at least monthly, compared with two-thirds of the general public.

The study also identified a demographic group known as "influentials." Influentials were the most socially and politically active group in the nation, and also the most recreationally active: nearly 9 out of 10 influentials engaged in outdoor activity once or more per month.

Outdoor Recreation Is Fun

There are many reasons that Americans give for participating in outdoor recreation. Some have to do with the social aspects—bonding with family and friends. Some have to do with fitness. Others have to do with a love of nature. But the number one reason given by Americans in the 1999 Roper survey was "to have fun" (83 percent). (See Figure 3.3.) The second-most popular reason was similar in nature: for relaxation (80 percent).

MOST POPULAR TYPES OF OUTDOOR ACTIVITY

The top five outdoor activities in 1999 were walking (42 percent), swimming (40 percent), driving for pleasure (35 percent), picnicking (32 percent), and fishing (28 percent). (See Table 3.3.) In fact, these were the top five activities for 1995 through 1999.

Participation in several outdoor activities increased from 1998 to 1999. Swimming experienced the biggest gains, with a 7 percent increase. Other categories in which participation increased sizably were fishing (6 percent) and campground camping (6 percent). Bike riding increased by 3 percent, and picnicking, recreational vehicle (RV) camping, motor boating, canoeing/kayaking, target shooting, motorcycling, horseback riding, mountain biking, and water-skiing each increased by 2 percent.

VISITING THE GREAT OUTDOORS

National and State Parks

One of the best ways to enjoy the outdoors is to visit the nation's National Park System (NPS). Since Congress established Yellowstone National Park as the first national park in 1872, the United States has created a system of national parks occupying millions of acres of land. Today, the 80-million-acre park system encompasses more than 369 parks, monuments, preserves, memorials, historic sites, recreational areas, seashores, and other units spread from Alaska to the U.S. Virgin Islands to American Samoa. In addition to providing recreation for almost 300 million visitors each year, the NPS preserves habitats that range from arctic tundra to tropical rain forest and protects many thousands of North American plant and animal species.

The park system is administered by the National Park Service. Established in 1916, the park service employs over

FIGURE 3.2

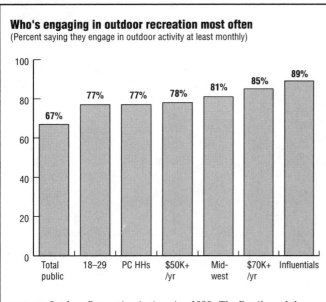

SOURCE: *Outdoor Recreation in America 1999: The Family and the Environment*, prepared for the Recreation Roundtable, Washington, D.C., by Roper Starch, 1999

FIGURE 3.3

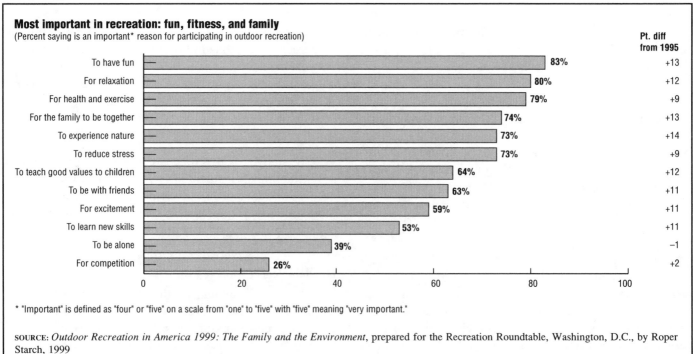

SOURCE: *Outdoor Recreation in America 1999: The Family and the Environment*, prepared for the Recreation Roundtable, Washington, D.C., by Roper Starch, 1999

TABLE 3.4

Types of areas administered by the NPS in 1998

Areas administered by type[1]	Recreation visits	Areas reporting visits	Areas not reporting	Areas administered
International Historic Site	0	0	1	1
National Battlefield Parks	2,107,177	3	0	3
National Battlefield Site	0	0	1	1
National Battlefields	1,432,180	10	1	11
National Historic Sites	10,410,358	70	6	76
National Historical Parks	25,198,829	34	4	38
National Lakeshores	4,098,943	4	0	4
National Memorials	29,415,352	27	1	28
National Military Parks	5,707,893	9	0	9
National Monuments	23,581,364	70	3	73
National Parks	64,461,974	53	1	54
National Parkways	32,816,485	4	0	4
National Preserves	1,571,878	15	1	16
National Recreation Areas	52,973,169	18	1	19
National Reserves	60,827	1	1	2
National Rivers	4,253,341	4	2	6
National Scenic Trails	0	0	3	3
National Seashores	18,521,892	10	0	10
National Wild and Scenic Rivers	1,051,956	5	4	9
Parks - Other[2]	9,075,497	10	1	11
NPS TOTAL	**286,739,115**	**347**	**31**	**378**

[1] Does not include 22 affiliated areas not reporting public use to the NPS. Does include Gloria Dei (Old Swedes') Church NHS as part of Independence NHS (not administered but reporting).

[2] Parks without national designation include National Capital Parks Central, National Capital Parks East, President's Park, Constitution Gardens, and White House.

SOURCE: *1998 Statistical Abstract,* National Park Service, Denver, CO, no date

12,000 permanent personnel and almost twice as many temporary or seasonal workers. Almost 99,000 volunteers spent vacation time working for the park service in 1997.

The NPS includes national parks, such as Yosemite National Park in California and Yellowstone National Park, mostly in Wyoming; national monuments, such as the Washington Monument and the Lincoln Memorial in Washington, D.C.; and national commemorative sites, such as the Gettysburg battlefield in Pennsylvania, the Vicksburg battlefield in Mississippi, and the Ellis Island Immigration Museum in New York. The NPS also includes some lakes, rivers, and seashores. (See Table 3.4 and Figure 3.4.)

Ten sites administered by the NPS accounted for 31 percent of all 1999 visits. (See Figure 3.5.) This was about the same as for 1997 (30 percent), when 275 million people visited NPS sites. Almost one in six adults (15 percent) took a trip of 100 miles or more to see a national park; 46 percent included a child or children on their trip. Among families with children living at home, 78 percent brought them to the parks. Men (49 percent) and women (51 percent) were equally likely to frequent the park system. Not surprisingly, park visitation was greatest in the summer months, peaking at 41.4 million visitations in July, and lowest in January (10.5 million).

In addition, many millions more visited national forests or lands administered by the Bureau of Land Management for car or motorcycle tours, camping, hunting, fishing, boating, and winter recreational activities. Others went to state parks and recreation areas.

Rails-to-Trails

Many railways around the country have been abandoned by the railroads. Almost every state has turned some of that acreage into public trails for hiking, jogging, biking, and even horseback riding. According to the Washington, D.C.–based Rails-to-Trails Conservancy, the 10 states that had done the most converting of trail mileage were Wisconsin (1,226 miles), Minnesota (1,174), Michigan (1,081), Pennsylvania (705), Iowa (495), Washington (440), New York (433), Maine (410), Illinois (367), and West Virginia (289).

BOATING

The National Marine Manufacturers Association (NMMA) estimated that, in 1998, 74.8 million Americans participated in recreational boating, fewer than the 78.4 million in 1997. Almost 17 million boats were in use, and 10 million people water-skied, down from 12 million in 1997. More than 12 million Americans were registered boaters. Michigan (957,105), California (894,347), Florida (796, 662), Minnesota (768,555), Texas (615,438), and Wisconsin (543,034) led in the number of registered boaters in 1997.

Americans owned about 1.6 million sailboats and approximately 2.4 million miscellaneous craft, such as

FIGURE 3.4

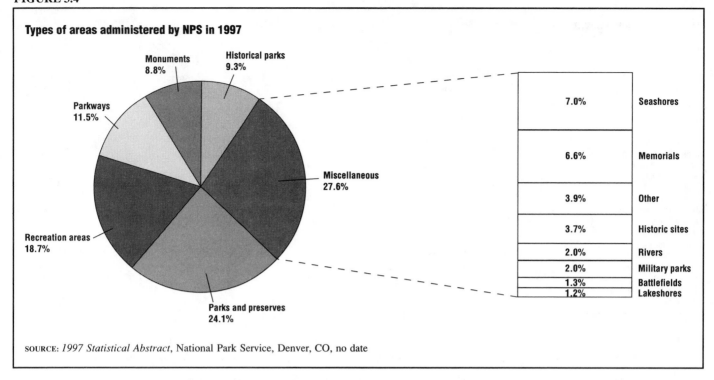

Types of areas administered by NPS in 1997

Monuments 8.8%

Historical parks 9.3%

Parkways 11.5%

Miscellaneous 27.6%

Recreation areas 18.7%

Parks and preserves 24.1%

7.0%	Seashores
6.6%	Memorials
3.9%	Other
3.7%	Historic sites
2.0%	Rivers
2.0%	Military parks
1.3%	Battlefields
1.2%	Lakeshores

SOURCE: *1997 Statistical Abstract*, National Park Service, Denver, CO, no date

FIGURE 3.5

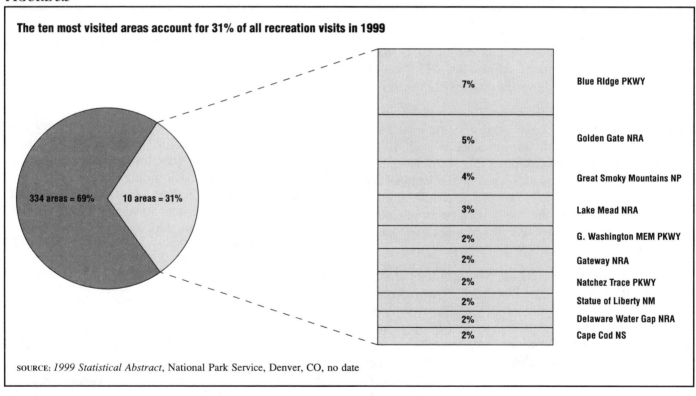

The ten most visited areas account for 31% of all recreation visits in 1999

334 areas = 69%   10 areas = 31%

7%	Blue Ridge PKWY
5%	Golden Gate NRA
4%	Great Smoky Mountains NP
3%	Lake Mead NRA
2%	G. Washington MEM PKWY
2%	Gateway NRA
2%	Natchez Trace PKWY
2%	Statue of Liberty NM
2%	Delaware Water Gap NRA
2%	Cape Cod NS

SOURCE: *1999 Statistical Abstract*, National Park Service, Denver, CO, no date

canoes and rowboats. There were 10,320 marinas, boatyards, yacht clubs, dockominiums, and parks in the United States in 1998, up from 10,128 in 1997. The NMMA estimated that Americans spent more than $19.1 billion on retail expenditures for boating in 1998, up from $13.7 billion in 1990. A U.S. Coast Guard survey found that Americans spent 7.7 billion hours boating in 1998.

GARDENING

According to the National Gardening Association (NGA), in 1994, almost three-fourths (72 million) of U.S. households had at least one gardener, down somewhat from 75 million in 1989. Gardening participation varies from year to year, based on homeownership rates, the number of sunny days during the growing season, and portrayals of gardening in popular movies. These people reported that they gardened for the pleasure of being outdoors, the aesthetic pleasure it provides, relaxation, and exercise.

Flower gardening is more popular than vegetable gardening in the United States. Four in 10 households grew flowers, compared with 3 in 10 for vegetables. Householders aged 35–54 (51 percent) were most likely to live in a flower-gardening household; middle-aged and older households were more likely to grow vegetables. On average, 31 percent of all households grew vegetables. The NGA predicted that the huge number of baby-boomer households entering the prime gardening ages would likely boost the overall number of flower-gardening households by 17 percent, and vegetable-gardening households by 18.5 percent, by 2010.

WILDLIFE AS RECREATION

America is a huge country with many millions of square miles of natural wilderness and has a rich tradition of enjoying nature. Many Americans find wildlife-associated recreation a source of immense pleasure, and some of the most popular recreational activities involve wildlife and wild places.

The 1999 Roper study found an increase, from 15 percent to 21 percent, in the number of Americans participating in campground camping. According to data published by the SGMA, Americans spent nearly 52 million days on overnight hiking/backpacking excursions. During 1999 the average participant went overnight hiking/backpacking on 8 occasions. Nearly 9 in 10 of the overnight hikers/backpackers also camped in tents. An American Sports Data study found that 21.6 million Americans aged 6 or older spent 15 days or more during 1998 engaged in outdoor activities such as camping, hiking, trail running, mountain/rock climbing, and similar activities. During 1999, 49.4 million U.S. residents went camping in a tent or recreational vehicle, and 12.8 million went canoeing. The SGMA reported that Americans purchased $1.765 billion in camping, hiking, backpacking, and other outdoor equipment during 1999.

National Survey

The mission of the U.S. Fish and Wildlife Service (FWS) is to conserve and enhance the nation's fish, wildlife, and habitat. For conservation efforts to be effective, the FWS needs to know how people use fish and wildlife resources. Since 1955 the FWS has conducted a periodic survey of fishing, hunting, and wildlife-related recreation.

The ninth report, the *1996 National Survey of Fishing, Hunting, and Wildlife-Associated Recreation* (U.S. Department of the Interior, Fish and Wildlife Service, and U.S. Department of Commerce, Washington, D.C., 1996), found that approximately 77 million Americans over the

FIGURE 3.6

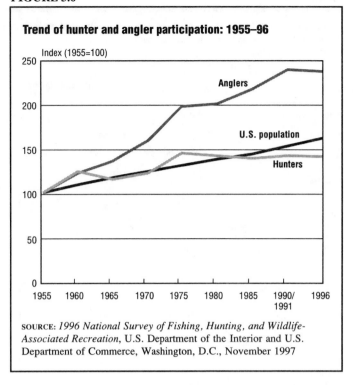

Trend of hunter and angler participation: 1955–96

SOURCE: *1996 National Survey of Fishing, Hunting, and Wildlife-Associated Recreation*, U.S. Department of the Interior and U.S. Department of Commerce, Washington, D.C., November 1997

age of 16 participated in some form of wildlife-related activity in 1996.

According to the survey, during 1996, 35.2 million people in the United States fished, 14 million hunted, and 62.9 million enjoyed some form of wildlife-watching recreation, including photographing or feeding animals. Among anglers (those who fish), hunters, and nonconsumptive participants (those who do not capture or kill the animals or fish as game), many of those who participated in one activity often enjoyed the other activities as well.

Trends

People are enjoying wildlife-related activities as much as ever. The number of anglers in 1996 (35.2 million) decreased only slightly since the all-time peak of 35.6 million in 1991. The number of hunters (14 million) remained about the same as in 1991, a 41 percent growth since 1955. (See Figure 3.6.) The number of people who took trips away from their homes to observe, feed, or photograph wildlife (23.7 million) fell by 12 percent from 1980 (the first year it was measured). The number of people who enjoyed these activities within 1 mile of their homes (60.8 million) dropped by 21 percent over that time.

Expenditures

In 1996 Americans spent about $101.2 billion on wildlife-related recreation. Fishing accounted for approximately 37 percent of that expenditure; wildlife-watching activities, 29 percent; and hunting, 20 percent. (Another 13 percent was unspecific.) Of the money spent, 60 per-

TABLE 3.5

Participants in wildlife-related recreation, by participant's state of residence: 1996

(Population 16 years old and older. Numbers in thousands)

Participant's state of residence	Population	Total participants		Sportsmen		Wildlife-watching participants	
		Number	Percent of population	Number	Percent of population	Number	Percent of population
U.S., total	201,472	76,964	38	39,694	20	62,868	31
Alabama	3,306	1,264	38	788	24	988	30
Alaska	432	279	65	187	43	216	50
Arizona	3,234	1,210	37	497	15	999	31
Arkansas	1,914	890	47	596	31	658	34
California	23,777	7,097	30	2,938	12	5,959	25
Colorado	2,929	1,535	52	732	25	1,244	42
Connecticut	2,514	928	37	375	15	774	31
Delaware	560	232	41	118	21	192	34
Florida	11,239	3,642	32	1,988	18	2,840	25
Georgia	5,544	1,960	35	1,093	20	1,622	29
Hawaii	900	201	22	136	15	123	14
Idaho	879	484	55	336	38	355	40
Illinois	8,979	3,740	42	1,761	20	3,137	35
Indiana	4,456	1,876	42	972	22	1,542	35
Iowa	2,174	1,032	47	607	28	828	38
Kansas	1,916	793	41	437	23	607	32
Kentucky	3,001	1,206	40	779	26	951	32
Louisiana	3,227	1,271	39	927	29	861	27
Maine	966	511	53	266	28	443	46
Maryland	3,912	1,537	39	629	16	1,323	34
Massachusetts	4,726	1,835	39	622	13	1,638	35
Michigan	7,267	3,134	43	1,748	24	2,585	36
Minnesota	3,473	1,663	48	1,212	35	1,325	38
Mississippi	2,032	680	33	519	26	458	23
Missouri	4,056	1,888	47	1,081	27	1,623	40
Montana	672	394	59	222	33	315	47
Nebraska	1,232	539	44	289	23	428	35
Nevada	1,214	365	30	223	18	258	21
New Hampshire	887	448	51	181	20	394	44
New Jersey	6,129	1,864	30	821	13	1,574	26
New Mexico	1,276	501	39	281	22	370	29
New York	13,944	3,800	27	1,708	12	3,169	23
North Carolina	5,605	2,364	42	1,217	22	1,984	35
North Dakota	483	190	39	148	31	112	23
Ohio	8,522	3,281	39	1,280	15	2,816	33
Oklahoma	2,484	1,199	48	798	32	860	35
Oregon	2,472	1,260	51	619	25	1,048	42
Pennsylvania	9,298	3,886	42	1,664	18	3,442	37
Rhode Island	759	284	37	111	15	243	32
South Carolina	2,842	1,093	38	718	25	829	29
South Dakota	541	249	46	204	38	165	30
Tennessee	4,120	1,792	44	820	20	1,507	37
Texas	14,186	4,695	33	2,772	20	3,553	25
Utah	1,396	558	40	331	24	415	30
Vermont	455	242	53	116	26	217	48
Virginia	5,168	2,278	44	1,090	21	1,905	37
Washington	4,207	1,908	45	1,018	24	1,621	39
West Virginia	1,467	593	40	374	26	452	31
Wisconsin	3,897	1,961	50	1,151	30	1,651	42
Wyoming	366	192	53	139	38	143	39

Note: Detail does not add to total because of multiple responses. U.S. totals include responses from participants residing in the District of Columbia.

SOURCE: *1996 National Survey of Fishing, Hunting, and Wildlife-Associated Recreation*, U.S. Department of the Interior and U.S. Department of Commerce, Washington, D.C., November 1997

cent was for equipment, 30 percent was trip-related, and 11 percent was "other."

Who Participates in Wildlife Sports?

The greatest number of wildlife enthusiasts lived in California, Texas, New York, Florida, Pennsylvania, Illinois, and Ohio. (See Table 3.5.) The greatest percentage

(24 percent) and the largest number of anglers and hunters were between the ages of 25 and 44. The majority of anglers and hunters were male: 73 percent of the anglers and 91 percent of the hunters. Of those who watched wildlife, 54 percent were female.

Most hunters (95 percent) were white, 2 percent were black, and 3 percent were other races. Among anglers, 90 percent were white, 5 percent were black, and 5 percent were other. Among those who participated in nonresidential wildlife-watching activities, 94 percent were white, 2 percent were black, and 7 percent were other.

Among anglers, 36 percent had a high school education, 24 percent had 1–3 years of college, and 27 percent had 4 years of college or more. Only 13 percent had fewer than 12 years of school. Among hunters, 41 percent had a high school diploma, 22 percent had 1–3 years of college, 22 percent had 4 years of college or more, and only 15 percent had fewer than 12 years of school. For those who enjoyed wildlife-watching activities, 27 percent had a high school diploma, 26 percent had 1–3 years of college, and 39 percent had 4 or more years of college. Only 7 percent had less than a high school education.

Hunting

In 1996, 14 million Americans 16 years and older enjoyed hunting a variety of game animals within the United States. In order of preference, hunters sought big game (deer, elk, bear, and wild turkey), small game (squirrels, rabbits, pheasants, quail, and grouse), migratory birds (doves, ducks, and geese), and other animals (groundhogs, raccoons, foxes, and coyotes). Hunters spent $20.6 billion on trips and equipment during the year. (See Table 3.6.) Collectively, they hunted 257 million days and took 223 million trips.

People living in the West North Central states were most likely to hunt (14 percent); residents of the Pacific states (4 percent) and the New England and Middle Atlantic states (5 percent each) were least likely. (See Figure 3.7.) Most people (51 percent) hunted on private land only; 30 percent, public and private; 17 percent, public only; and 2 percent were unspecified.

Animal rights advocates have criticized hunters as wanton, unfeeling killers. Hunters and hunters' organizations are working to counter that image by teaching ethics to hunters, promoting the contributions that hunters make to conservation, and defending hunting as a tradition as old as time. The campaign to clean up hunting's reputation comes as a few states have restricted some types of hunting—baiting of bears in Michigan and Washington and airborne hunting of wolves in Alaska.

Fishing

In 1996 more than 35.2 million U.S. residents enjoyed a variety of fishing activities throughout the United States. Collectively, anglers fished 626 million days and took 507 million fishing trips. Freshwater species were fished for by 84 percent of anglers; saltwater fish were fished for by 26 percent. (There was some overlap due to the anglers who fished for both.) Anglers spent $38 billion on fishing-related expenses during the year. Of that

TABLE 3.6

Total hunting expenditures

Total trip-related	**$ 5.2 billion**
Food and lodging	2.5 billion
Transportation	1.8 billion
Other trip costs	0.9 billion
Total equipment expenditures	**$11.3 billion**
Hunting equipment	5.5 billion
Auxiliary equipment	1.2 billion
Special equipment	4.5 billion
Total other hunting expenditures	**$4.1 billion**
Magazines, books	0.1 billion
Membership dues and contributions	0.2 billion
Land leasing and ownership	3.2 billion
Licenses, stamps, tags, and permits	0.7 billion
Total hunting expenditures	**$20.6 billion**

SOURCE: *1996 National Survey of Fishing, Hunting, and Wildlife-Associated Recreation*, U.S. Department of the Interior and U.S. Department of Commerce, Washington, D.C., November 1997

amount, 41 percent was trip-related, 51 percent went for equipment, and 9 percent was for other expenses.

Wildlife-Watching Activities

Wildlife-watching activities, including observing, feeding, and photographing wildlife, continue to be popular in the United States. These activities are considered as being either residential (within a mile of one's home) or nonresidential (at least 1 mile from home). In 1996, 31 percent (62.9 million) of the American population 16 years and older enjoyed watching wildlife. They spent an average of $554 per participant. Of the total spent, 57 percent was for equipment, 32 percent was trip related, and 11 percent went for other expenses.

Among the 61 million people who enjoyed wildlife-watching activities in their own communities (residential), 86 percent fed the birds, 73 percent observed wildlife, 32 percent fed other wildlife, 26 percent photographed wildlife, and 18 percent visited public areas, such as parks, within 1 mile of their homes. Another 15 percent maintained plantings for wildlife, while an additional 13 percent maintained natural areas for the primary purpose of benefiting wildlife. (See Figure 3.8.) Among those who took trips away from home for the primary purpose of observing, feeding, or photographing wildlife, 97 percent observed, 51 percent photographed, and 42 percent fed the animals.

Residents from the West North Central (35 percent), East North Central (34 percent), and New England (35 percent) areas of the country were most likely to enjoy local wildlife activities. (See Figure 3.9.) Residents of the Mountain states (16 percent) were most likely to travel to participate in wildlife activities. (See Figure 3.10.) Almost equal proportions of males and females enjoyed wildlife-watching activities.

FIGURE 3.7

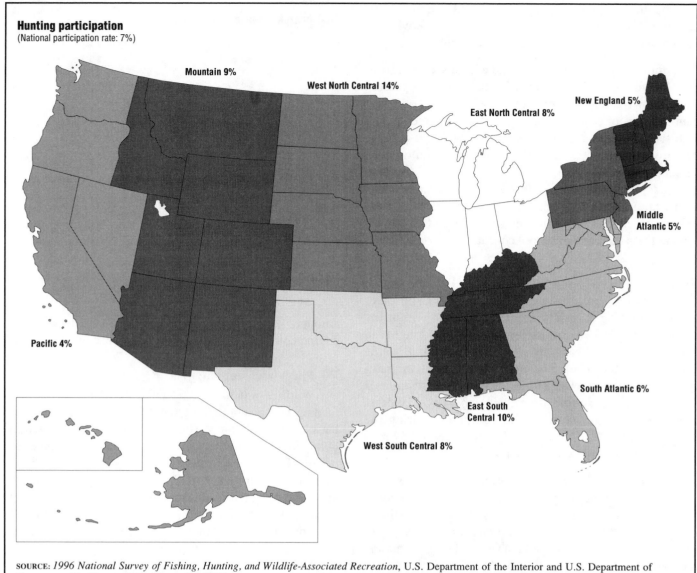

Hunting participation
(National participation rate: 7%)

Mountain 9%

West North Central 14%

East North Central 8%

New England 5%

Middle Atlantic 5%

Pacific 4%

East South Central 10%

West South Central 8%

South Atlantic 6%

SOURCE: *1996 National Survey of Fishing, Hunting, and Wildlife-Associated Recreation*, U.S. Department of the Interior and U.S. Department of Commerce, Washington, D.C., November 1997

Whale Watching

Whale watching became increasingly popular in the 1990s. The whales support an industry pouring millions into many coastal economies. The Whale and Dolphin Conservation Society, based in Bath, England, reported that, in 1994, 5.4 million people in 65 countries went on whale-watching expeditions, and the number was growing by 10 percent each year. Two-thirds of whale watching was done in the United States. Worldwide, the activity generated more than $500 million in revenue.

Whale watching in the United States brought an estimated $37.5 million in direct revenue and another $155.5 million in associated businesses. In southern New England alone, tourists paid more than $21 million each year to visit whales in their natural environment. Humpback, fin, minke, and, occasionally, orca or pilot whales frequented these waters, and the highly endangered North Atlantic right whale could sometimes be seen.

The California gray whale, now removed from the endangered species list, was the star of the West Coast's whale-watching industry. Commercial whale-watching vessels also served as forums for educational outreach and scientific research.

"Canned Hunting"

In the 1990s a controversial form of commercial exploitation of wildlife, known as canned hunting, swept across the country. Beginning in Texas, canned hunting now occurs in most states. A 1994 Humane Society investigation found that there may be as many as several thousand canned-hunting facilities in the United States.

In a canned hunt, the "hunter" pays a set fee and steps into an enclosure where an animal—boar, ram, bear, lion,

FIGURE 3.8

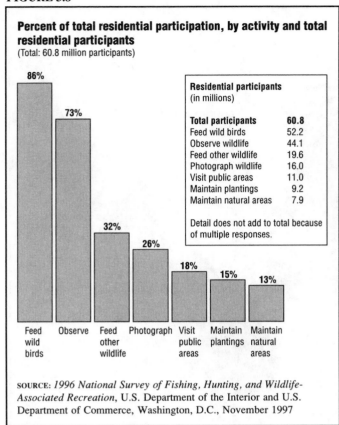

Percent of total residential participation, by activity and total residential participants
(Total: 60.8 million participants)

Residential participants (in millions)	
Total participants	**60.8**
Feed wild birds	52.2
Observe wildlife	44.1
Feed other wildlife	19.6
Photograph wildlife	16.0
Visit public areas	11.0
Maintain plantings	9.2
Maintain natural areas	7.9

Detail does not add to total because of multiple responses.

SOURCE: *1996 National Survey of Fishing, Hunting, and Wildlife-Associated Recreation*, U.S. Department of the Interior and U.S. Department of Commerce, Washington, D.C., November 1997

tiger, zebra, buffalo, rhinoceros, or antelope—is confined. The hunter then kills the animal with the weapon of his or her choice. The animals are easily cornered. Some have been domesticated or raised in facilities where they have become friendly to humans, even walking up to them.

No federal laws restrict canned hunts. Wisconsin and California are the only two states that have laws governing canned hunts. Investigations reveal that zoos across the nation have sold animals they consider surplus either directly to canned-hunt facilities or to dealers who sell animals to auctions patronized by canned-hunt organizers. Some pressure has been exerted on zoos to acknowledge their responsibility for the animals they discard.

MOTORCYCLING—CHANGING TIMES

Motorcycling is not only a means of transportation but also a popular recreational activity. The Motorcycle Industry Council reported, in its *1998 Motorcycle Statistical Annual* (1998), that motorcycle sales peaked in 1970, when more than 1.1 million new units were sold. In 1980, 1 million were sold, and the number declined until the early 1990s. Sales of new bikes were up 4–5 percent from 1992 to 1995, 6.8 percent in 1996, and 8 percent in 1997, when 356,000 motorcycles were sold. In 1997 an estimated 6.5 million motorcycles were in use in the United States by 5.16 million motorcycle owners.

The Motorcycle Owner—A Profile

In 1980 the average age of registered motorcyclists was 26; by 1990, 32; and by 1998, 38. In 1980 the average motorcycle owner earned $17,500 per year; by 1990, $33,100; and in 1998, $44,100.

According to Mediamark Research, a New York market research firm, in 1998, almost 60 percent of all motorcycle owners were between the ages of 35 and 64. Nearly half earned more than $50,000 a year, and nearly 25 percent made salaries above $75,000. Today, the industry increasingly caters to aging baby boomers with disposable income and a "yen" for adventure. Manufacturers have introduced a line of bigger, safer, more expensive machines with plenty of extras—wide-body, big-windshield cruising bikes—aimed at customers more interested in comfort than performing daredevil acrobatics.

One in four motorcycles sold today is sold to a woman. Very expensive bikes are bringing the industry back. The recovery of Harley-Davidson from the edge of bankruptcy was based on marketing to older, more affluent consumers looking for excitement in their lives.

RECREATIONAL VEHICLES

Recreational vehicles (RVs) include a variety of vehicles, such as motor homes, travel trailers, folding camping trailers, truck campers, and van conversions. Motor homes and vans are motorized, while the others must be towed or mounted on other vehicles. (See Figure 3.11.) There are approximately 9.3 million RVs in the United States—1 in every 10 vehicle-owning households. There are an estimated 30 million RV enthusiasts, including renters of RVs.

RV sales peaked in the mid- to late 1970s. The Recreational Vehicle Industry Association reported that in 1978 shipments totaled 389,900 units. A declining economy around 1980 dragged sales to 107,200. Since then, sales have climbed steadily. In 1997, 254,500 RVs were shipped.

Who Owns RVs?

The mainstay purchaser of an RV has traditionally been the older, high-wage blue-collar worker. Ownership rates are highest in the 55–74 age group. Only an estimated one-fourth of RV owners buy RVs new, showing how expensive they can be and the importance of the resale RV market.

Shifting U.S. demographics—the aging of baby boomers—will likely add to the growth of the RV industry. Increasing numbers of single people, especially women, are also taking to the road in RVs.

AMUSEMENT AND THEME PARKS AND CIRCUSES

Theme and amusement parks, in general, enjoyed growth in attendance in the 1990s. According to Economic

FIGURE 3.9

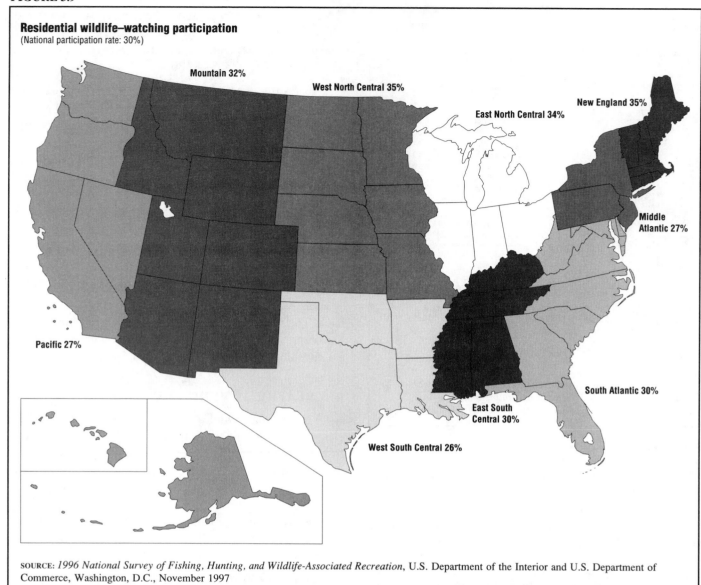

Residential wildlife–watching participation
(National participation rate: 30%)

Mountain 32%

West North Central 35%

East North Central 34%

New England 35%

Middle Atlantic 27%

Pacific 27%

South Atlantic 30%

East South Central 30%

West South Central 26%

SOURCE: *1996 National Survey of Fishing, Hunting, and Wildlife-Associated Recreation*, U.S. Department of the Interior and U.S. Department of Commerce, Washington, D.C., November 1997

Consulting Services of Newport Beach, California, attendance at the nation's top 50 parks increased 3.6 percent annually, to almost 161 million people. Most of that growth, however, was due to the opening of new parks, such as Universal Studios and Disney's MGM Studio, both in Florida, and Six Flags Fiesta Texas in San Antonio, Texas. Overall attendance increases obscure the diminishing popularity of theme parks, especially among middle-aged and older adults. In 1990, 28 percent of adults 18 and older reported they had visited a theme park in the previous 12 months; in 1997, 26 percent said they had done so.

Many adults may be wearying of the very things that give young adults such a thrill: high-tech, action-packed adventure. In addition, theme parks are becoming increasingly expensive to attend. Estimated per capita expenditures at the nation's top 50 parks grew dramatically—72 percent—from 1987 to 1997; in 1997 the average visitor spent $33.82.

Because children usually go with an adult to such parks, theme parks are looking for ways to appeal to adult visitors. The parks of the future will likely anticipate the wants and needs of these older customers. They will feature fewer high-tech rides and put more emphasis on serene, comfortable surroundings, such as fountains, seats, and beautiful scenery.

Women, who have their own money to spend today, prefer less violent and more family-oriented activities. Parks are expected to cater to those preferences as well. Legoland, which opened in Carlsbad, California, in 1998, is a place where visitors build structures with blocks, and appeals to women and families for that reason. Tivoli Gardens, in Denmark, features scenic gardens and fountains. Experts say that competition in the entertainment industry is heavy, and theme and amusement parks will have to change in coming years to keep their adult customers happy.

FIGURE 3.10

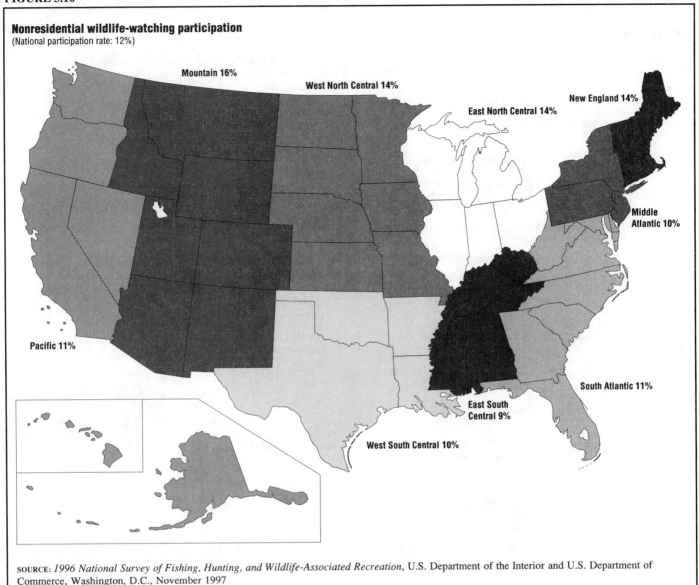

Nonresidential wildlife-watching participation
(National participation rate: 12%)

Mountain 16%

West North Central 14%

East North Central 14%

New England 14%

Middle Atlantic 10%

Pacific 11%

South Atlantic 11%

East South Central 9%

West South Central 10%

SOURCE: *1996 National Survey of Fishing, Hunting, and Wildlife-Associated Recreation*, U.S. Department of the Interior and U.S. Department of Commerce, Washington, D.C., November 1997

Thrills on the Midway—From Wild to Wired

Like much of American technology, amusement park rides have gone high-tech. Computers now control the operations of rides, making the job of a ride operator much like that of flight attendants—they make sure the automatic safety bars are secure and that possessions are stowed away. The computer systems are designed to operate without rest and with the utmost precision.

Ringling Brothers Comes to Town

According to company spokesperson Susannah Smith, Ringling Brothers Circus, the "Greatest Show on Earth," plays to more people than any other live show—11 million people a year—and appears within 100 miles of 87 percent of the American population. Each of Ringling's two touring groups travels to more than 90 cities during a two-year run.

In 1995 Ringling launched its first-ever advertising campaign. For generations, before the advent of radio and television, Ringling Brothers advertising was the spectacle itself, a Pied Piper strategy designed to draw the public into the circus tent. Essentially, the circus sold itself. Today, however, circus officials find themselves competing with many other entertainment venues. In response, the company began direct marketing (sending brochures to customers on a mailing list) and promotions in local newspapers and television stations, supermarkets, department stores, and other retailers. It also began affixing its name to video games, snack foods, and baby products.

THRILL CHASING—"EXTREME SPORTS"

Growing numbers of people are participating in high-risk recreational activities. Young adults dominate the thrill seekers, but older people are jumping in, too.

FIGURE 3.11

RV types and terms

Recreation vehicle/RV (AR'-Vee)n.— A recreation vehicle, or RV, is a motorized ot towable vehicle that combines transportation and temporary living quarters for travel, recreation and camping. RVs do not include mobile homes, off-road vehicles or snowmobiles. Following are descriptions of specific types of RVs and their average retail price.

TOWABLES
An RV designed to be towed by a motorized vehicle (auto, van, or pickup truck) and of such size and weight as not to require a special highway movement permit. It is designed to provide temporary living quarters for recreational, camping or travel use and does not require permanent on-site hook-up.

$14,200
Conventional travel trailer
Ranges typically from 12 feet to 35 feet in length, and is towed by means of a bumper or frame hitch attached to the towing vehicle.

$22,600
Fifth-wheel travel trailer
This unit can be equipped the same as the conventional travel trailer but is constructed with a raised forward section that allows a bi-level floor plan. This style is designed to be towed by a vehicle equipped with a device known as a fifth-wheel hitch.

$5,000
Folding camping trailer
A recreational camping unit designed for temporary living quarters which is mounted on wheels and connected with collapsible sidewalls that fold for towing by a motorized vehicle.

$11,000
Truck camper
A recreational camping unit designed to be loaded onto or affixed to the bed chassis of a truck, constructed to provide temporary living quarters for recreational camping or travel use.

MOTORIZED
A recreational camping and travel vehicle built on or an integral part of a self-propelled motor vehicle chassis. It may provide kitchen, sleeping, and bathroom facilities and be equipped with the ability to store and carry fresh water and sewage.

$75,000
Motor home (Type A)
The living unit has been entirely constructed on a bare, specially designed motor vehicle chassis.

$43,000
Van camper (Type B)
A panel type truck to which the RV manufacturer adds any of the two following conveniences: sleeping, kitchen and toilet facilities. Also 110/120-volt hook-up, fresh water storage, city water hook-up and a top extension to provide more head room.

$47,000
Motor home (Type C)
This unit is built on an automotive manufactured van frame with an attached cab section. The RV manufacturer completes the body containing the living area and attaches it to the cab section.

$27,000
Conversion vehicles
Vans, trucks and sport utility vehicles manufactured by an automaker then modified for transportation and recreation use by a company specializing in customized vehicles. These changes may include windows, carpeting, paneling, seats, sofas, and accessories.

SOURCE: Recreational Vehicle Industry Association. Available at: http://www.rvia.org/consumers/recreationvehicles/types.htm

---

Skydiving, hang gliding, rock climbing, mountaineering, bungee jumping, whitewater rafting, and other risky sports are all showing huge increases in participation. The U.S. Bungee Association estimated that, in 1997, there had been 7 million bungee jumps worldwide since the late 1980s. The sport was growing fastest in South America.

The U.S. Parachute Association (USPA) reported that its membership was more than 34,000 in 2001 and growing. Between 130,000 and 150,000 people skydive every year. The USPA reported that most skydivers were younger men, but the numbers of women and older persons were growing rapidly; the fastest-growing group was the 40-plus group. Twenty-two percent of members

were in their forties; 7 percent, their fifties; and 7 percent, 60 and older.

The American Mountain Guides Association reported a membership of 620 in 2001, with steady growth. Mountain climbing has become so popular that getting away from the crowd can be difficult. Some mountain climbers have reported scaling remote peaks only to find other climbers there. Even on Mount Everest, the tallest mountain in the world, a number of teams might be active on the slopes at any one time. Participation is growing among nontraditional groups, and rock-climbing gyms have sprung up around the country. Women can excel in climbing because flexibility and balance can be more important than muscle bulk.

One explanation for the rising popularity of "extreme sports" is the rising awareness created by the media. Movies and advertising often feature mountain climbers or skydivers. In addition, many participants report a life affirming "adrenaline rush," and some experts suggested that participants in dangerous activities enjoyed the appearance of living on the edge. These people often like to "break the rules," be extraordinary, and do what others only dream of. They are quickly bored. Industry experts call these people "experiencers."

As a result, advocates of extreme sports continue to search for new challenges. Skydiving now has new forms, including sky surfing, free-flying, and aerial ballet, for those who think simply jumping from 15,000 feet is too easy. Bungee jumping now includes "BASE"—bridge, aerial, structure, and earth jumping.

Other experts believe that the growing participation in extreme sports has much to do with increasing income levels, lifestyle changes, and improved safety of extreme sports due to technology and training. Technology can build a bungee cord or a parachute almost certainly not likely to fail, and modern sports medicine can both recommend exercises to prepare participants for the sport and treat them after a mishap.

Selling Excitement

Advertisers of products, such as sport-utility vehicles, largely targeted to Generation Xers—who account for most "experiencers"—have found they must present their products as fun items for breaking the rules. (For more information on recreation expenses, see Chapter 2.)

Experts predict that the popularity of extreme sports will grow as baby boomers' earnings continue to rise. Furthermore, traditional obstacles to participation, such as gender and age, are fast disappearing, as people stay physically active longer.

Less Risky Extremes

Now that extreme sports are "in," recreation researchers classify certain difficult or somewhat dangerous outdoor activities as "extreme." Some of these activities are relatively new, and some have been around for a while. The SMGA released results, based upon its 1999 study on sports participation, of the top 10 most popular extreme sports in the United States. Number one was in-line skating, with 27.8 million participants. (See Table 3.7.) Interestingly, this figure dropped significantly from the 1998 level of participation (32 million) according to SGMA statistics. The second-most popular extreme sport, mountain biking (7.8 million), also experienced a drop from 1998 levels of participation (8.6 million).

TABLE 3.7

Most popular extreme sports in the USA
(6 years of age or older)

Sport	# of participants (participated at least once in 1999)	"Frequent" participants
1. In-line skating	27,865,000	9,087,000 (25+ days/year)
2. Mountain biking	7,849,000	1,998,000 (25+ days/year)
3. Skateboarding	7,807,000	1,480,000 (52+ days/year)
4. Paintball	6,364,000	1,172,000 (15+ days/year)
5. Artificial wall climbing	4,817,000	N/A
6. Snowboarding	4,729,000	653,000 (15+ days/year)
7. BMX bicycling	3,730,000	1,052,000 (52+ days/year)
8. Wakeboarding	2,707,000	568,000 (15+ days/year)
9. Mountain/rock climbing	2,103,000	N/A
10. Surfing	1,736,000	N/A

SOURCE: "Whassup...with Extreme Sports," Sporting Goods Manufacturers Association, North Palm Beach, FL, October 30, 2000

Does this mean "extreme" is no longer fashionable? Not necessarily. The 1999 participation rates for skateboarding (7.8 million), paintball (6.3 million), artificial wall climbing (4.8 million), wakeboarding (2.7 million), and mountain/rock climbing (2.1 million) all were higher than the figures reported by SGMA for 1998. As in all things, tastes and fashion in recreation change with the times.

THE FUTURE OF OUTDOOR RECREATION

According to the middle-series projections of the Census Bureau, the total population of the United States will increase 54 percent between 1990 and 2050. Most of the growth, however, will be among the older ages and minorities, neither of which have high participation in active sports. A rapidly increasing share of young adults will be black, Hispanic, or Asian. In general, minorities have less discretionary income than whites, especially older whites.

Steve Murdock of Texas A&M University, in *An American Challenge: Population Change and the Future of the United States* (1996), predicted that bird-watching (58.5 percent) was the only outdoor activity in which the number of participants would grow faster than the population growth (54 percent). According to Murdock, walking, the most frequently enjoyed outdoor activity in 1990, would likely increase by 52.2 percent. The participation of blacks, Hispanics, and other minorities should increase rapidly in every sport because these races will dominate younger cohorts who have the highest sports-participation rates. Young minorities, however, have fewer financial resources, and the slowest-growing sports, such as backpacking and tennis, appeal mostly to the young and affluent. The long-term status of any sport, Murdock contended, will likely depend on the number of minority participants.

CHAPTER 4
THE ARTS AND MEDIA

ATTENDING ARTS ACTIVITIES

More Americans are attending arts activities. The National Endowment for the Arts survey, *1997 Survey of Public Participation in the Arts (SPPA),* found that half the American adult population, or 97 million people, attended at least one of seven arts activities—jazz, classical music concerts, operas, musical plays, plays, ballets, or art museums. In contrast, in 1992, only 41 percent of adults participated in the arts.

Visiting art museums was a popular activity. An estimated 35 percent of adults visited a museum at least once in the preceding year, followed by musical plays (25 percent), nonmusical plays (16 percent), classical music con-

certs (16 percent), jazz (12 percent), ballet (6 percent), and opera (5 percent). (See Table 4.1.) The average person visited art museums more than three times, for a total of 225 million visits.

In addition, a number of related arts activities had high participation rates. Of adults, 63 percent said they had read literature (such as plays, poetry, and short stories), and 47 percent had visited a historic park or an arts and crafts fair. (See Table 4.1.)

In general, attendance at various arts events was highest among whites, except for jazz events—which African Americans attended in greater proportions—and opera and art museums, which drew a higher proportion of

TABLE 4.1

Attendance at arts events: 1997

Arts activity	Persons		Attendances / visits	
	Percent of adults participating at least once in last 12 months	Number of adults attending/visiting in millions[1]	Average number of visits per attender	Total number of visits in millions
Attended				
Jazz performance	11.9%	23.3	3.1	72.2
Classical music	15.6	30.5	2.9	88.5
Opera performance	4.7	9.2	1.8	16.5
Musical play	24.5	47.9	2.2	105.4
Non-musical play	15.8	30.9	2.5	77.3
Ballet	5.8	11.3	1.7	19.3
Other dance[2]	12.4	24.3	2.6	63.1
Visited				
Art museum	34.9	68.3	3.3	225.3
Historic park	46.9	91.7	4.1	376.1
Art/craft fair	47.5	92.9	2.6	241.6
Read				
Literature[3]	63.1	123.4	NA[4]	NA[4]

[1] The number of attenders was computed by multiplying the attendance rate by 195.6 million: the U.S. resident noninstitutionalized population, 18 years of age and over in 1997.
[2] "Other dance" refers to dance other than ballet, including, for example, modern, folk and tap.
[3] "Literature" refers to reading plays, poetry, novels or short stories.
[4] No frequency information was obtained for reading literature.

SOURCE: *1997 Survey of Public Participation in the Arts,* National Endowment for the Arts, Washington, D.C., 1998

TABLE 4.2

Attendance rates for various arts activities

(In percent. For persons 18 years old and over. Excludes elementary and high school performances. Based on the 1997 household survey Public Participation in the Arts. Data are subject to sampling error)

Item	Attendance at least once in the prior 12 months at -								
	Jazz perfor-mance	Classical music perfor-mance	Opera	Musical play	Non-musical play	Ballet	Art museum	Historic park	Reading literature[1]
Total	12	16	5	25	16	6	35	47	63
Sex:									
Male	13	14	4	22	15	4	34	48	55
Female	11	17	5	27	17	8	36	46	71
Race:									
Hispanic	7	8	3	16	10	5	29	33	50
White	12	18	5	27	17	7	36	51	65
African American	16	10	2	22	16	4	31	37	60
American Indian	11	9	5	15	5	1	22	42	56
Asian	10	16	7	20	18	4	42	44	69
Age:									
18 to 24 years old	15	16	5	26	20	7	38	46	70
25 to 34 years old	13	11	4	23	13	5	37	49	61
35 to 44 years old	14	14	4	26	15	7	37	52	64
45 to 54 years old	13	20	6	29	20	7	40	54	66
55 to 64 years old	9	16	5	23	14	5	30	45	58
65 to 74 years old	8	18	4	24	15	5	28	37	59
75 years old and over	4	14	3	15	13	4	20	25	61
Education:									
Grade school	2	2	-	6	3	2	6	13	29
Some high school	3	4	2	13	7	2	14	27	46
High school graduate	7	8	2	16	9	4	25	41	58
Some college	15	18	5	28	19	7	43	56	72
College graduate	21	28	10	44	28	11	58	67	80
Graduate school	28	45	14	50	37	14	70	73	86
Income:									
$10,000 of less	5	4	2	12	10	2	16	23	45
$10,001 to $20,000	6	8	2	12	7	3	20	29	53
$20,001 to $30,000	8	10	2	17	10	4	26	39	62
$30,001 to $40,000	11	13	3	21	16	5	32	50	62
$40,001 to $50,000	11	15	5	23	15	6	37	52	64
$50,001 to $75,000	16	22	8	32	20	8	46	62	72
$75,001 to $100,000	23	26	6	41	27	10	55	65	75
Over $100,000	27	35	13	51	32	13	60	69	76

[1] Includes novels, short stories, poetry, or and plays.

SOURCE: *1997 Survey of Public Participation in the Arts*, U.S. National Endowment for the Arts, Research Division Note #70, July 1998

Asians. People between the ages of 45 and 54 were somewhat more likely to go to such events. The more education people had, and the greater their income, the more likely they were to attend. (See Table 4.2.)

The *Art Newspaper,* a London-based international monthly magazine, in its annual survey of visitors to art exhibitions in North America, Europe, and Australia, also reported that American art museums were experiencing a boom. The survey found, as it had in 1998, that "the keenest visitors" to art exhibits during 1999 were the Americans. Not only were attendance figures high for museums in New York, Los Angeles, and Washington, D.C., but Boston, Atlanta, Seattle, and Chicago made the top 20 as well.

The most visited show during 1999 was "Van Gogh's Van Goghs" at the Los Angeles County Museum of Art, with 821,004 visitors (7,017 per day). This is all the more impressive when you consider that top daily attendance figures during 1998 were the Washington, D.C., premiere of "Van Gogh's Van Goghs" (5,339 per day) and "Monet in the Twentieth Century" at the Boston Museum of Fine Art (5,290 per day).

Creating Art

The SPPA also asked respondents about their *doing* of art—personally performing or creating art. The study found the highest rates of personal participation were in photography (17 percent), painting/drawing (16 percent), dance other than ballet (13 percent), creative writing (12 percent), and classical music (11 percent). Also, in 1997 more than 10 percent of the adult population sang publicly in a choir, chorus, or other ensemble. The lowest rates were in jazz and opera (2 percent each) and in ballet (less than 1 percent). (See Table 4.3.)

TABLE 4.3

Participation in the arts via personal performance and creation: 1997

Arts activity	Private and/or public performance/display		Public performance, display, or publication	
	% of adults doing at least once in last 12 months	Number of adults doing (millions)[1]	% of adults doing at least once in last 12 months	Number of adults doing (millions)[1]
Playing				
Jazz	2.2%	4.3	0.9%	1.8
Classical music	11.0	21.5	1.3	2.5
Singing				
Opera	1.8	3.5	0.3	0.6
Musicals	7.7	15.1	1.7	3.3
Choirs, chorale	NA[2]	NA[2]	10.4	20.3
Dancing				
Ballet	0.5	1.0	0.3	0.6
Other dance	12.6	24.6	2.0	3.9
Acting in non-musical plays	NA[2]	NA[2]	2.7	5.3
Painting/drawing	15.9	31.1	2.9	5.7
Pottery	15.1	29.5	2.4	4.7
Weaving	27.6	54.0	2.7	5.3
Buying art	35.1	68.7	NA[3]	NA[3]
Photography	16.6	32.6	2.3	4.5
Creative writing	12.1	23.7	1.2	2.3
Composing music	3.7	7.2	1.3	2.6

[1] The number of personal participants was computed by multiplying the participation rate by 195.6 million: the U.S. resident noninstitutionalized population, 18 years of age and over.
[2] For these activities, questions were only asked about public performances.
[3] For this activity only questions about "doing" were asked.

SOURCE: *1997 Survey of Public Participation in the Arts,* National Endowment for the Arts, Washington, D.C., 1998

Whites and Asians (12 percent each) were more likely to play classical music than American Indians (9 percent), blacks (8 percent), or Hispanics (7 percent). Greater percentages of blacks bought artwork (43 percent) and sang in groups (26 percent) than Asians (19 percent bought artwork and 9 percent sang in groups), whites (36 percent bought artwork and 8 percent sang in groups), or Hispanics (33 percent bought artwork and 7 percent sang in groups). American Indians pursued modern dancing (21 percent), pottery (25 percent), and photography (28 percent) more than other races. Asians outnumbered other races in creative writing (21 percent) and drawing (27 percent). In general, active participation in artistic endeavors declined with age.

Spending on Art Activities

In addition to increased participation in the arts, Americans are spending more on the arts. According to data released by the Bureau of Economic Analysis, a division of the U.S. Department of Commerce, Americans spent $9.4 billion on admissions to performing arts events in 1998. This included admissions to both nonprofit and for-profit organizations, such as Broadway theater and rock concerts.

THEATER, CONCERTS, AND OPERAS

Before there were movies, television, and radio, there was theater. The first American theater, with actors, scenery, and numerous play productions, came to the American colonies from England in 1750. By the beginning of the nineteenth century, every major city had a theater to put on plays.

Taking the Show on the Road

As the American population grew and spread westward, so did the number of theaters. From New York City, the leading theater center, hundreds of theater companies took their performers on the road to bring entertainment to new settlers all across the country. Until the early 1900s, the theater—which included opera, drama, comedy, and musical shows—was America's main form of entertainment. An original American theater type was the showboat, which sailed up and down the Mississippi River entertaining passengers and the gamblers who made a living on the river.

Broadway

The modern period on Broadway began in New York City with the founding of the Theater Guild in 1918. It was the first commercially successful art theater to produce plays that were equal to the high-quality productions of those in Europe. Other theaters soon opened and did very well until the stock market crash of 1929. The nation recovered from the Great Depression that followed, but theater did not, because more and more people were going to the motion pictures or staying home to listen to the radio or, later, watch television or rented movies.

It has become extraordinarily expensive to put on a Broadway show. In many cases, the exciting special effects are more important than the play. In the show *Sunset Boulevard,* there are two separate stages. In *Miss Saigon,* a real helicopter lands on the stage. As a result, fewer and fewer shows are being produced on Broadway. In 1980 there were 61 new Broadway shows; by 1991 just 28 new shows had started; and in 1996, 38 plays. In 1996, 9.5 million people spent $436 million to see the shows on Broadway.

Nonprofit Theater

In 1996 about 228 nonprofit theater companies existed in the United States, down slightly from 231 in 1994. Theater groups include ensembles, touring companies, children's theater, and small companies. They perform the classics, modern plays, musicals, new plays by American and foreign playwrights, experimental works, and plays aimed at young audiences. In 1980, 14.2 million people attended nonprofit theater productions; in 1994, 20.7 million attended; and in 1996, 17.1 million attended.

When Americans have less money to spend, fewer people go to the theater, and private donors contribute less. If the cost of putting on productions increases at the same time, some nonprofit theater groups are forced to close.

Going to Concerts and Operas

In 1996, 31.1 million people went to hear 28,887 concerts of all types. That same year, 6.5 million people attended the 2,296 performances put on by the nation's 83 opera companies.

MEDIA USAGE

Americans devote much time to the media, which include television, radio, recorded music, newspapers, books, magazines, home video, movies in theaters, video games, and online computer services. In general, the less costly a form of consumer media, the greater the media usage. Broadcast TV and radio are free to consumers and are the most widely used media. Subscription video services are next in terms of cost and popularity, followed by recorded music and online services. The most expensive media on an hourly basis are movies in theaters and home video.

Fairfield Research reported that, in 1998, Americans spent 13 percent more time with media than they did in 1995. The average adult spent 3,368 hours—69 percent of his or her waking hours—consuming media in one form or another that year. Consumption of interactive media was up 100 percent, and that of the print media—magazines, newspapers, trade publications, and books—grew 21 percent, while TV viewing declined 18 percent.

MOVING PICTURES—THE BIRTH OF AN INDUSTRY

In 1891 Thomas Alva Edison, the American inventor best known for the electric light bulb and phonograph, or talking machine, applied for a patent on a "kinetoscopic camera." This camera took motion pictures on a band of film that could be seen by looking or "peeping" into a box, which gave these early pictures the name "peep shows." This box soon developed into movie projectors and screens. In 1893 Edison and his partner, W. K. L. Dickson, built the Black Maria, the first movie studio.

As America moved into the twentieth century, such inventions as the automobile, radio, telephone, and airplane were beginning to change the way people lived. While not everyone could afford all the modern wonders, almost anyone could pay the price of a ticket to see "moving pictures" wherever there was a theater and a piano to play the background music. (The first motion pictures had no sound, and the actors' words were printed on the screen so the audience could follow the plot. A piano player added music to make the movie more exciting.)

The first "blockbuster" movie, *The Birth of a Nation,* released in 1915, upset some Americans because it was racist. World War I (1914–18) gave filmmakers something audiences wanted to see, and the American Film Institute Catalog lists 1,175 war films made during that time. The first "talking picture" was the 1927 *The Jazz Singer.* The years following World War I were years of financial growth for the United States, and this helped the motion picture industry to become very successful. By the mid-1920s, some 20,000 movie theaters were showing moving pictures in the United States, twice the number of theaters as in 1910.

Movie Business Boom

Motion pictures remained one of America's favorite pastimes throughout the 1930s and 1940s. By 1950 television had become the new developing technology. As television grew in popularity, fewer people went to the movies. Weekly movie attendance dropped from about 90 million people in 1947 to an average of 42 million in the 1950s and 1960s. Gross sales fell from an all-time record high of $1.5 billion in 1957 to a yearly average of $1.2 billion in the 1950s and rose only slightly in the 1960s.

To meet the threat of television, movie producers in the 1950s introduced many types of three-dimensional (3-D) movies to lure people to the movies. Special glasses had to be worn for 3-D movies to make figures "jump off" the screen.

In 1945 there were 20,355 movie houses; by 1960 that number had dwindled to 11,300. On the other hand, 4,700 drive-in movies were built during the 1950s. These outdoor theaters meant families could drive up to speakers and view the movies on giant screens while sitting in the comfort of their own cars. Drive-ins solved baby-sitting problems for parents and were so popular they accounted for 25 percent of movie attendance in 1950s. As suburbs spread out and property became more expensive, theater

TABLE 4.4

Per capita personal expenditures on performing arts events, motion pictures, and spectator sports: 1993–98

	1998 $billions		1997 $billions		1996 $billions		1995 $billions		1994 $billions		1993 $billions	
	Nominal	Real	Nominal	Real	Nominal	Real	Nominal	Real	Nominal	Real	Nominal	Real
Admission receipts to specified entertainments	$88.05	$83.61	$82.92	$80.67	$78.06	$78.06	$73.07	$76.87	$69.92	$76.87	$67.90	$76.43
Performing arts	$34.78	$32.93	$32.49	$31.37	$30.17	$30.17	$28.92	$30.45	$27.66	$29.97	$26.38	$29.87
Motion pictures	$25.16	$24.05	$23.90	$23.16	$21.87	$21.87	$20.93	$22.07	$19.98	$21.90	$19.40	$21.73
Spectator sports	$28.12	$26.64	$26.52	$25.77	$26.02	$26.02	$23.21	$24.36	$22.28	$24.20	$22.11	$24.44

Note: "Real" refers to estimates that are measured in 1996 chained dollars to control for inflation.

SOURCE: Research Division Note #75, National Endowment for the Arts, March 2000

companies started to build theaters that would show many movies at the same time. The number of drive-ins began to fall. By 1971 the number of drive-ins had fallen to 3,720, and, today, only a handful remain in the whole country.

Personal movie theater attendance remained relatively constant in the 1990s, at about 12 hours per person per year. Consumer spending on movies in theaters rose slightly from $19.40 per person in 1993 to $25.16 in 1998. (See Table 4.4.) Like spectator sports and the performing arts, motion picture admission receipts per capita have increased steadily but modestly since 1993. (See Figure 4.1.)

Adults aged 18–24 (34 percent) were significantly more likely than average to go to the movies at least once a month than all adults (20 percent). Although members of that age group have much lower incomes than their older counterparts, they also have fewer financial responsibilities. Moviemakers, therefore, generally make movies aimed to please younger audiences.

Young adults, however, were going to the movies less often than in previous decades due to competition from videotapes, video games, and computers. The movie industry might not be able to count on young audiences to fill theaters. It is, therefore, trying to expand its audience by making more movies with older stars and mature plots. Some theaters are also trying new marketing techniques, such as combining dinner and a movie under one roof.

VIDEOCASSETTE RECORDERS

Some experts believed that videocassette recorders (VCRs), which make it so easy to watch movies at home, would hurt movie box-office sales more than television. Many others thought that VCRs would make more money for a film. Moviemakers now know that if a movie makes money at the box office, it will also make money with video sales. In fact, sometimes a bad movie will not even be shown at the movie house and will be sent directly to video stores, where it may earn some money. VCR sales have become just as important as domestic and foreign sales to the financial success of a film.

FIGURE 4.1

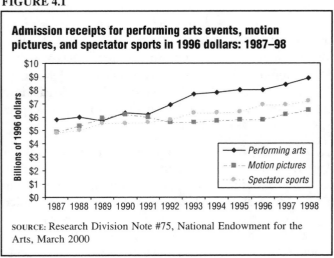

Admission receipts for performing arts events, motion pictures, and spectator sports in 1996 dollars: 1987–98

SOURCE: Research Division Note #75, National Endowment for the Arts, March 2000

Media Dynamics reported that, in 1996, 82.2 percent of U.S. households—79 million homes—had VCRs, compared with 1.1 percent in 1980. Americans spent, on average, 49 hours per person per year watching home videos. Nearly 23 percent of Americans watched a rented video on a regular basis, and 36 percent sometimes watched videos. About 11 percent hardly watched a video, while 30 percent never did. The total time watching tapes could be even greater, but apparently only half of all home-recorded programs are ever played back. By 1998, 91 percent of Americans had a VCR.

A 1999 Gallup survey found that watching movies at home was the seventh-most popular way for Americans to spend an evening. Those choosing home movie viewing as their favorite evening activity (7 percent), however, were still fewer than those who said that going to the movies or theater was their favorite way to spend an evening (11 percent).

TELEVISION

Television has defined two generations of consumers. It does not, however, possess the unifying power it once had. A TV watcher in decades past could tune in to Milton Berle or *Gunsmoke* and know he was sharing the moment with nearly every other American. Today, people have many more choices, including cable TV, satellite TV, pay-per-view, rented videotapes, and computers. The American viewing audience has become fragmented.

Television is the most used of media forms, which also include home video, radio, CD/tape, magazine, newspaper, book, and PC/World Wide Web. In 1997 Americans watched 1,561 hours of television per person, approximately 3.75 hours per day, slightly less than 1,567 hours per person in 1996. A 1999 Nielsen Media Research report found that virtually all U.S. households had at least one TV and three-quarters of all households had more than one TV. Many Americans leave the TV on whether or not they happen to be watching it at any given moment. During a day, the TV in American households is on an average of seven hours. During March 1999, Nielsen found that about 97 million Americans per day watched TV during prime time (Monday–Saturday, 8 P.M. to 11 P.M. EST; Sunday, 7 P.M. to 11 P.M. EST). Because so many Americans have the TV on, over $45 billion is spent each year by TV advertisers.

Although watching TV was the most popular way for Americans to spend an evening according to a 1999 Gallup poll, there were demographic differences in viewing habits. For example, TV viewing was found to be much less popular among young people than among older Americans. Of persons 65 years of age or older, 60 percent said watching TV was their favorite way to spend an evening, compared with 21 percent of persons aged 18–29. In addition, TV watching is more popular among groups with lower levels of education. Better-educated Americans tend to have greater interest in reading or dining out.

Effect of the Internet on TV Viewing

A Gallup poll suggested that the Internet might be decreasing the amount of time spent in front of the TV. The Gallup organization found that 28 percent of Americans watched more than four hours of TV per day, an increase from 23 percent in 1985. Nevertheless, the number of persons who watched between three and four hours of TV per day fell from 37 percent in 1985 to 29 percent at the beginning of 2000. The percentage of people watching less than three hours per day increased from 35 percent in 1985 to 42 percent in 2000.

The evidence of the Internet's effect on TV viewing is mixed. A 1999 study by the Stanford Institute for the Qualitative Study of Society found that 60 percent of Internet users said that the Internet had reduced their TV viewing. One-third said that it had reduced the amount of time they spent reading the newspaper. Nielsen's 1999 research study, however, found only about a 10 percent reduction in the number of hours a TV was on in an Internet household,

compared with a non-Internet household. During prime time, there was little difference at all between Internet households and non-Internet households. The greatest difference in TV usage was during the daytime.

Cable and Satellite Television

Cable television subscribers pay a monthly fee to cable companies to receive not only regular broadcast channels, but also such specialized channels as MTV, a music video channel; Nickelodeon, a children's channel; and ESPN, a sports channel. Cable TV subscribers who choose to pay more can also see the latest movies on such channels as HBO or Showtime. For the first time, in 1995, basic cable channels drew slightly more total viewers than the three biggest networks (ABC, CBS, and NBC) in homes that had cable. During prime-time hours, however, the networks still had more viewers than the cable channels.

According to a 1999 Nielsen Research Study, three-quarters of Americans had access to cable or satellite TV. By 1998 the average home with one of these systems was able to receive 57 channels. People who subscribed to premium services watched, on average, 15 hours per week more TV than people who did not subscribe to premium services. Although the number of channels available is large, viewers tended to select certain channels that they watched repeatedly. The average number of channels watched for 10 or more consecutive minutes was 13.

NEWS VIEWERSHIP—REMOTE CONTROL IN HAND

The average American dedicates more than an hour a day to the news. More read, watch, or listen to the news than exercise or use a personal computer. Although Americans are reading, listening to, and watching the news as often as in the past, technological change and the news climate have changed the way they do so. Television news is in trouble with the American public. Fewer and fewer people are watching network broadcasts for news coverage. The Pew Research Center's *Biennial News Consumption Survey: Internet News Takes Off* (1998) found that Americans were increasingly turning to the Internet for news coverage. The number of Americans seeking news coverage online tripled from 1995 to 1998—from 11 million to 36 million users. Those who went online for news coverage were younger, better educated, and more affluent. (See Table 4.5.)

The number of people watching cable news coverage now approximates the audience for network programming, with 40 percent of Americans regularly watching cable news, compared with 57 percent who view network news. The size of the cable news audience swells to 60 percent when specialty programs, such as the Weather Channel and ESPN's Sports Center, are included.

TABLE 4.5

Percent of all adults who go online to get news at least once a week

	1995	1998	Change
Total	4	20	+16
Gender			
Men	6	25	+19
Women	3	15	+12
Race/ethnicity			
White	4	20	+16
Black	3	14	+11
Hispanic	6	18	+12
Age			
18–29	7	30	+23
30–49	5	24	+19
50–64	2	13	+11
65+	1	4	+3
Education			
College graduate	10	35	+25
Some college	6	25	+19
H.S. graduate	2	11	+9
Less than H.S.	1	11	+10
Family income			
Over $50,000	8	34	+26
$30,000–$49.999	5	22	+17
$20,000–$29,999	3	14	+11
Under $20,000	1	8	+7

SOURCE: *Pew Research Center Biennal News Consumption Survey,* The Pew Research Center for the People and the Press, Washington, D.C., 1998

TABLE 4.6

Younger Americans:
Turned on by information, off by news

	18–29	30–49	50–64	65+
Like having so many information sources to chose from	77%	70%	64%	52%
Enjoy keeping up with the news a lot	33%	48%	59%	68%

SOURCE: *Pew Research Center Biennal News Consumption Survey,* The Pew Research Center for the People and the Press, Washington, D.C., 1998

Cable's advantage lies in its immediacy. Americans said they would turn to cable channels first in the event of a major news story. National news is followed by 46 percent of Americans only when something major is happening, and 63 percent react the same way to international news. Only local news attracts a large regular audience that is not event-driven—61 percent of Americans follow it most of the time. The percentage of Americans who viewed only network and local TV news fell from 30 percent in 1993 to 15 percent in 1998.

The study also found that young Americans were not as interested in the news as older Americans. Only 33 percent of Americans 18–29 said they enjoyed keeping up with the news, compared with 68 percent of seniors (ages 65 and older). (See Table 4.6.)

The Weather Channel and ESPN are very popular. Fully 33 percent of the public watched the Weather Channel regularly, and another 27 percent watched sometimes. Of adults, 20 percent watched ESPN sports regularly.

HOME ELECTRONICS PRODUCTS

America's love affair with consumer electronics shows no sign of waning. Cellular phones, camcorders, cordless phones, large-screen TVs, and high-definition television (HDTV) sets are high on the wish lists of many Americans. In 1998 retailers said they expected to sell as many HDTVs as the industry could make, despite price tags of more than $8,000 and their huge size.

The Consumer Electronics Manufacturers Association (now called the Consumer Electronics Association) estimated, in *U.S. Consumer Electronics Sales and Forecasts: 1994 to 1999* (1999), that the typical American household spent $1,000 per year on consumer electronics. U.S. consumers have invested more than $407 billion on approximately 1.6 billion electronic products. Americans spent $76 billion on consumer electronics in 1998 alone.

Since 1985 the number of wireless telephone subscribers has skyrocketed, according to the Cellular Telecommunication Industry Association. In 1990 approximately 500,000 Americans used cellular phones; in 1995, about 28 million persons; and by 1998, 60 million.

Americans cannot get enough of consumer electronics. Sales of combination TV/VCRs increased by 14 percent during 1998. Compact audio system sales increased by 13 percent that same year, and sales of digital cameras grew by 57 percent. Digital video products were expected to grow an average of 35 percent per year through 2002.

Figure 4.2 illustrates the extent to which consumer electronics are a part of Americans' everyday life. According to the Consumer Electronics Association, as of June 1998, 98 percent of American homes had color TV. Almost as many (91 percent) had a VCR. Seventy-three percent had a cordless phone and nearly as many (71 percent) had a telephone answering machine. Over half (54 percent) had a CD player. More than 2 out of 5 households had a personal computer (44 percent), wireless phone (41 percent), and computer printer (41 percent). About 3 out of 10 had a camcorder (32 percent), computer with CD-ROM (30 percent), pager (29 percent), electronic car alarm (29 percent), and modem or fax/modem (29 percent); 1 in 5 households had a home theater system.

RECORDED MUSIC

Americans are the heaviest purchasers of recorded music in the world. The Recording Industry Association

FIGURE 4.2

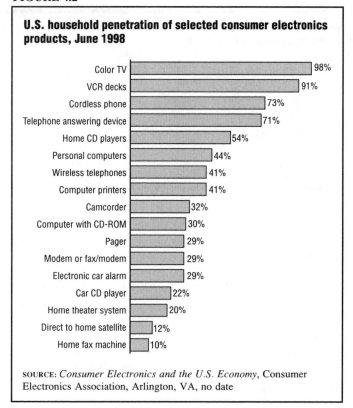

U.S. household penetration of selected consumer electronics products, June 1998

Product	Penetration
Color TV	98%
VCR decks	91%
Cordless phone	73%
Telephone answering device	71%
Home CD players	54%
Personal computers	44%
Wireless telephones	41%
Computer printers	41%
Camcorder	32%
Computer with CD-ROM	30%
Pager	29%
Modem or fax/modem	29%
Electronic car alarm	29%
Car CD player	22%
Home theater system	20%
Direct to home satellite	12%
Home fax machine	10%

SOURCE: *Consumer Electronics and the U.S. Economy*, Consumer Electronics Association, Arlington, VA, no date

of America, a trade association, reported that the total U.S. dollar value of audio recordings nearly doubled during the 1990s, growing from $7.5 billion in 1990 to $14.5 billion in 1999. The dollar value increased every year during the decade, except in 1997 when it decreased slightly compared with 1996 figures.

The most popular category of music was rock, at 25.2 percent. (See Table 4.7.) The popularity of rock, however, changed over the decade. In 1990, 36.1 percent of audio-recording consumers purchased rock music. This percentage fell steadily over the next few years to 30.2 percent in 1993. There was a resurgence in rock music purchases in 1994 (35.1 percent), but then another steady decline to 32.5 percent in 1997.

A dramatic change occurred in 1998. Rock dropped from 1997's figure to 25.7 percent. During that same year, there were increases in the percentage of persons purchasing religious music (from 4.5 percent to 6.3 percent) and "other" (from 5.7 percent to 7.9 percent).

During the 1990s, the category of "other," which includes spoken word, exercise, humor, ethnic, and other types of audio recordings, nearly doubled, increasing from 5.6 percent in 1990 to 9.1 percent in 1999. Conversely, the percentage of persons buying New Age music fell by more than half, from 1.1 percent in 1990 to half a percent in 1999. Purchases of jazz recordings dropped, also, from 4.8 percent in 1990 to 3 percent in 1999. Pop fell from 13.7 percent to 10.3 percent and purchases of

religious music more than doubled, from 2.5 percent to 5.1 percent.

The form in which Americans purchased music also changed. In 1990 most audio recordings purchased were cassette tapes (54.7 percent). By 1999 cassette purchases had dropped to 8 percent. CDs became the format of choice, rising from 31.1 percent in 1990 to 83.2 percent in 1999.

Older Americans made a high percentage of audio recording purchases. In 1990 only 11.1 percent of audio recordings were purchased by Americans 45 years of age and older. By 1999 that figure had more than doubled to 24.7 percent. Particularly noteworthy during the 1990s was that the percentage of purchases made by consumers aged 15 through 19 dropped from 18.3 percent in 1990 to 12.6 percent in 1999. These trends perhaps reflected the aging of the baby boomer generation.

Americans no longer rely as much on record stores to supply their music. In 1990 nearly 7 out of 10 music purchases were made in record stores. By 1999 only 44.5 percent of such purchases were made in record stores. Over 38 percent of music purchases were made in stores other than record stores. Only a small percentage of people (2.4 percent) purchased music over the Internet during 1999, but that was more than double the percentage of such purchases made in 1998, perhaps an indicator of things to come.

During the 1990s, gender differences in purchasers pretty much evened out. In 1990 most music purchases (54.4 percent) were by males. In 1999 males made 50.3 percent of the purchases and females 49.7 percent.

THE INTERNET AND CONVERGENCE

An explosion in digital technology coupled with growth of the Internet make the possibilities for media experience in the future breathtaking. It may soon be possible to move from one medium to another in the same delivery platform—TVs or personal computers. Statistics from IntelliQuest showed that 83 million Americans over age 16 accessed the Internet in 1999, an increase from 66 million in 1998. Of these, 3.7 million were using hand-held computers and 3.1 million were using a television set-top box or WebTV.

A 1999 survey of Internet users by America Online and Roper Starch found that 44 percent of them felt that "going online is increasingly becoming a necessity." Sixty-nine percent felt it was important for children to go online, indicating a recognition that the Internet will be of extreme importance for the next generation. Over three-quarters (77 percent) said that the Internet had improved their life. Seventy-one percent said that they researched purchases on the Internet and 42 percent said they made

TABLE 4.7

Music buyer profile, 1999

	1990	1991	1992	1993	1994	1995	1996	1997	1998	1999
Total U.S. dollar value*	$7,541.1	$7,834.2	$9,024.0	$10,046.6	$12,068.0	$12,320.3	$12,533.8	$12,236.8	$13,723.5	$14,584.5
Rock	36.1%	34.8%	31.6%	30.2%	35.1%	33.5%	32.6%	32.5%	25.7%	25.2%
Country	9.6	12.8	17.4	18.7	16.3	16.7	14.7	14.4	14.1	10.8
Rap/hip hop[1]	8.5	10.0	8.6	9.2	7.9	6.7	8.9	10.1	9.7	10.8
R&B/urban[2]	11.6	9.9	9.8	10.6	9.6	11.3	12.1	11.2	12.8	10.5
Pop	13.7	12.1	11.5	11.9	10.3	10.1	9.3	9.4	10.0	10.3
Religious[3]	2.5	3.8	2.8	3.2	3.3	3.1	4.3	4.5	6.3	5.1
Classical	3.1	3.2	3.7	3.3	3.7	2.9	3.4	2.8	3.3	3.5
Jazz	4.8	4.0	3.8	3.1	3.0	3.0	3.3	2.8	1.9	3.0
Soundtracks	0.8	0.7	0.7	0.7	1.0	0.9	0.8	1.2	1.7	0.8
Oldies	0.8	1.0	0.8	1.0	0.8	1.0	0.8	0.8	0.7	0.7
New Age	1.1	1.3	1.2	1.0	1.0	0.7	0.7	0.8	0.6	0.5
Children's	0.5	0.3	0.5	0.4	0.4	0.5	0.7	0.9	0.4	0.4
Other[4]	5.6	4.2	5.4	4.6	5.3	7.0	5.2	5.7	7.9	9.1
Full Length Cassettes	54.7	49.8	43.6	38.0	32.1	25.1	19.3	18.2	14.8	8.0
Full Length Cds	31.1	38.9	46.5	51.1	58.4	65.0	68.4	70.2	74.8	83.2
Vinyl Lps	4.7	1.7	1.3	0.3	0.8	0.5	0.6	0.7	0.7	0.5
Singles (all types)	8.7	8.8	7.5	9.2	7.4	7.5	9.3	9.3	6.8	5.4
Music Videos	NA	0.4	1.0	1.3	0.8	0.9	1.0	0.6	1.0	0.9
10–14 years	7.6	8.2	8.6	8.6	7.9	8.0	7.9	8.9	9.1	8.5
15–19 years	18.3	18.1	18.2	16.7	16.8	17.1	17.2	16.8	15.8	12.6
20–24 years	16.5	17.9	16.1	15.1	15.4	15.3	15.0	13.8	12.2	12.6
25–29 years	14.6	14.5	13.8	13.2	12.6	12.3	12.5	11.7	11.4	10.5
30–34 years	13.2	12.5	12.2	11.9	11.8	12.1	11.4	11.0	11.4	10.1
35–39 years	10.2	9.8	10.9	11.1	11.5	10.8	11.1	11.6	12.6	10.4
40–44 years	7.8	6.7	7.4	8.5	7.9	7.5	9.1	8.8	8.3	9.3
45+ years	11.1	11.8	12.2	14.1	15.4	16.1	15.1	16.5	18.1	24.7
Recond store	69.8	62.1	60.0	56.2	53.3	52.0	49.9	51.8	50.8	44.5
Other store	18.5	23.4	24.9	26.1	26.7	28.2	31.5	31.9	34.4	38.3
Tape/record club	8.9	11.1	11.4	12.9	15.1	14.3	14.3	11.6	9.0	7.9
Mail order	2.5	3.0	3.2	3.8	3.4	4.0	2.9	2.7	2.9	2.5
Internet[5]	NA	NA	NA	NA	NA	NA	NA	0.3	1.1	2.4
Female	45.6	45.9	47.4	49.3	47.3	47.0	49.1	51.4	51.3	49.7
Male	54.4	54.1	52.6	50.7	52.7	53.0	50.9	48.6	48.7	50.3

* These figures (in millions) indicate the overall size of the U.S. sound recording industry based on manufacturers' shipments at suggested list prices.
1 "Rap/Hip Hop": Includes Rap (8.8%) and Hip Hop (2.0%).
2 "R&B/Urban": Includes R&B, Blues, Dance, Disco, Funk, Fusion, Motown, Reggae, Soul.
3 "Religious": Includes Christian, Gospel, Inspirational, Religious, and Spiritual.
4 "Other": Includes Ethnic, Standards, Big Band, Swing, Latin, Electronic, Instrumental, Comedy, Humor, Spoken Word, Exercise, Language, Folk, and Holiday Music.
5 "Internet": Does not include record club purchases made over the Internet.

SOURCE: Recording Industry Association of America, Washington, D.C., no date

purchases on the Internet. Experienced Web surfers had spent an average of $226 on purchases via the Internet during the previous three months and new users had spent about half as much ($109).

Children in particular increasingly view the Internet as a necessity. In the same survey, 63 percent of Internet-using children said they preferred the Web to TV. Over half (55 percent) said they would rather go online than talk on the phone. Children aged 9 through 11 said they logged on an average of three times a week and children aged 15 through 17 said they logged on an average of five days per week.

Internet Access—The Digital Divide

Opinions differ concerning how demographic factors affect access to the Internet. A report from the Department of Commerce, *Falling through the Net: Defining the Digital Divide,* used data collected by the Census Bureau in 1997–98 from 48,000 households across America. The report found that people with college degrees were more than 16 times as likely to have Internet access at home as persons with only an elementary education.

High-income households in urban areas were 20 times as likely to have Internet access as low-income, rural households. In low-income households, the report found that children in white families were three times as likely as children in black households, and four times more likely than children in Hispanic households, to have Internet access.

A 1999 study by the Stanford Institute for the Qualitative Study of Society, however, reached different conclusions. The study's authors found that income, race,

TABLE 4.8

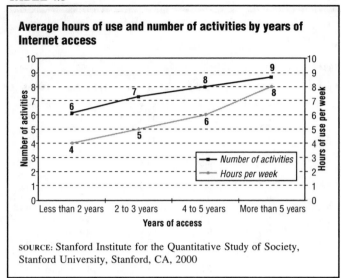

Average hours of use and number of activities by years of Internet access

SOURCE: Stanford Institute for the Quantitative Study of Society, Stanford University, Stanford, CA, 2000

ethnicity, and gender had a statistically insignificant effect on access. The most important factors affecting Internet access, according to the study, were age and education. For example, the study found that a college education increased rates of Internet access by more than 40 percentage points compared with the least educated group. Similarly, a drop of over 40 percentage points in rate of Internet access was seen for people over age 65, as compared with people less than 25 years of age. The Stanford study concluded that youth and education were the key factors in Internet access.

For those with access, the Stanford study found that there were few demographic differences in the amount of use of the Internet. The most important difference, which suggested that the importance of the Internet would only increase in the future, was how long Internet users had been connected to the Internet. As indicated in Figure 4.3, both hours of use and number of Internet activities increase the longer someone is an Internet user.

READING: THE OLDEST MEDIA OF ALL

Notwithstanding all of the interest and excitement about new media, a 1999 Gallup poll found that Americans continued to read as much as they had for the previous 20 years. Claiming to have read more than 50 books during the prior year, 7 percent of Americans were avid readers.

Age and race appeared to have little impact on reading habits, according to the Gallup poll results. The most important factor likely to increase how much Americans read was the amount of education they had. Six percent of readers were in book discussion groups.

CHAPTER 5
FOOTBALL, BASEBALL, BASKETBALL, AND OTHER POPULAR SPORTS

Many Americans love sports, and most schoolchildren grow up playing team and individual sports as part of their physical education. Many men have played baseball or softball at some time in their lives, and some continue to play in community or neighborhood leagues long after they are finished with school. Today, women are playing sports once played mainly by men, such as soccer, baseball, and basketball. Many, many men and women are sports fans.

SPECTATOR SPORTS

In March 2000 a Gallup poll asked Americans what was their favorite sport to watch. Of respondents, 33 per-

cent said football; 16 percent, basketball; 13 percent, baseball; and 5 percent each for golf, ice hockey, and auto racing. (See Table 5.1.) For the first year since 1948, in 1997, basketball surpassed baseball. Since 1990 golf has slowly overtaken tennis. (See Table 5.2.)

Historically, football, baseball, and basketball have been called the "holy trinity" of sports in the United States. They make money not only by filling ballparks and arenas with fans, but also from televised sports events. The start of each new sports season brings hope to millions of sports fans that their team will be in the championship game at the end of the season. These sports also fill stadiums with fans to watch middle and high school, collegiate, and professional games.

In 1996, 61.7 million people attended major league baseball games. In 1996 almost 21.7 million spectators came out to watch Michael Jordan, Jason Kidd, Shaquille O'Neal, and other National Basketball Association stars play. Even more (28.2 million) went to see National Collegiate Athletic Association (NCAA) men's college basketball, and 5.2 million cheered for women's college

TABLE 5.1

What is your favorite sport to watch?

	2000 Mar	1998 Nov	1997 Apr**	1995 Apr	1994 Sep	1994 Aug
Football	33%	36%	30%	32%	37%	35%
Basketball	16	12	17	15	13	11
Baseball	13	16	14	16	16	21
Ice hockey	5	3	3	3	1	3
Golf	5	3	5	4	3	3
Auto racing	5	3	7	2	2	2
Ice/figure skating	4	2	2	2	3	3
Soccer	2	2	2	1	2	2
Boxing	2	1	2	1	1	1
Tennis	1	2	2	2	3	2
Wrestling	1	1	1	1	*	1
Gymnastics	1	1	1	0	0	*
Bowling	*	1	*	1	*	*
Fishing	*	1	*	1	*	*
Swimming	*	—	—	—	—	—
Horse racing	—	*	1	0	0	*
Other	3	6	6	7	5	5
None	8	9	6	10	12	10
No opinion	1	1	1	2	2	1
	100%	100%	100%	100%	100%	100%

* Less than 0.5%
** Question wording: What is your favorite sport to follow?

SOURCE: *The Gallup Poll Monthly*, April 1997, The Gallup Organization, Princeton, NJ, 1997

TABLE 5.2

Favorite spectator sport: trends

	Football	Baseball	Basketball	Tennis	Golf
1997 Apr 18–20	30	14	17	2	5
1995 Apr 17–19	32	16	13	2	4
1994 Sep	37	16	13	3	3
1994 Aug	35	21	11	2	3
1992 Sept	38	16	12	5	3
1990 Feb	35	16	15	3	2
1981	38	16	9	—	—
1972	36	21	8	—	—
1960	21	34	9	—	—
1948	17	39	10	—	—

SOURCE: *The Gallup Poll Monthly*, April 1997, The Gallup Organization, Princeton, NJ, 1997

FIGURE 5.1

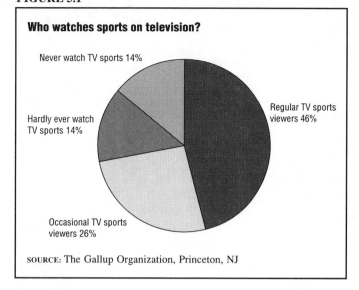

Who watches sports on television?

Never watch TV sports 14%

Hardly ever watch TV sports 14%

Regular TV sports viewers 46%

Occasional TV sports viewers 26%

SOURCE: The Gallup Organization, Princeton, NJ

TABLE 5.3

Most popular sports for men based on "frequent" participation
(Age 6 and older; in thousands)

Activity	1999
1. Recreational walking (52+ days/year)	14,799
2. Basketball (25+ days/year)	12,397
3. Fishing (15+ days/year)	10,362
4. Recreational bicycling (52+ days/year)	9,986
5. Free weights: barbells (100+ days/year)	7,510
6. Recreational swimming (52+ days/year)	7,148
7. Calisthenics (100+ days/year)	7,108
8. Free weights: dumbbells (100+ days)	7,102
9. Stretching (100+ days/year)	6,894
10. Running/jogging (100+ days)	6,252

SOURCE: *Men are still Flexing their Muscles,* Sporting Goods Manufacturers Association, North Palm Beach, FL, July 31, 2000

basketball. More than 17 million fans attended hockey games in 1996, while 43.3 million went to horse races. In 1998 audiences nationwide watched as Mark McGwire and Sammy Sosa chased Roger Maris's home-run record. In 2001 millions of fans around the country watched the Super Bowl victory of the Baltimore Ravens over the New York Giants in one of the country's biggest media events—"Super Bowl Sunday."

Most people do not go to the stadium to watch their favorite team play; they watch on television. A 1995 Gallup poll found that nearly 46 percent of the American public watched basketball, baseball, or football regularly on TV; 26 percent watched sometimes; 14 percent hardly ever watched; and another 14 percent never watched. (See Figure 5.1.)

Professional Wrestling—Is It a Sport?

Professional wrestling enjoyed an increase in popularity in the 1990s. A 1999 Gallup poll found that almost 2 of 10 Americans (18 percent) considered themselves wrestling fans. Wrestling is no longer limited to regular professional wrestling TV shows. The World Wrestling Federation and World Championship Wrestling make millions of dollars every year from pay-per-view events.

Wrestling fans tended to be males with a high school education who earned less than $30,000 per year. The percentage of wrestling fans who were over 30 years of age or who had a college education was very low. Of blacks, 39 percent considered themselves to be wrestling fans, compared with 16 percent of whites.

Professional wrestling is really athletic entertainment, since the results of the match are usually predetermined, a fact many Americans formerly did not understand. The 1999 survey found that 8 out of 10 Americans believed the outcomes of most wrestling matches were fixed, compared with less than 2 of 10 who believed that in 1951.

Perhaps this accounts for why 81 percent of Americans, according to the survey, said that wrestling was not a sport. True wrestling fans, however, beg to differ. Among persons calling themselves wrestling fans, 44 percent said that wrestling was, indeed, a sport.

THE WEEKEND WARRIOR—SPORTS PARTICIPATION

Every year, American Sports Data surveys individuals in 15,000 households about their favorite sports and sports activities for the Sporting Goods Manufacturers Association (SGMA). In 1999 the top three activities were recreational swimming, walking, and bicycling. Bowling was the fourth-most popular sport. Except for basketball, the other sports in the top 10 of popularity were fitness or outdoor activities. (See Table 1.6 in Chapter 1.)

Gender Differences

For both men and women, the most popular sport was recreational walking. (See Tables 5.3 and 5.4.) Women walkers, however, outnumbered their male counterparts by almost two to one. Nearly 24 million women walked for recreation, compared with fewer than 15 million men.

Basketball was the second-most popular sport among men, with 12.4 million frequent participants in 1999. Basketball was the seventh-most popular sport among women, with 4.6 million frequent participants. Basketball was the only team sport among the top 10 sports participated in frequently by either men or women. Frequent participation in basketball, however, declined for both sexes compared with 1997 figures.

Fishing was decidedly a preference of men more than women. It was the third-most popular sport for men to participate in frequently, but did not make the top 10 for women. Approximately 10.4 million men fished 15 or more days during 1999.

Recreational swimming was popular both for men and women. More women (9.6 million) than men (7.1 million) engaged in recreational swimming during 1999. Most other top 10 sports engaged in frequently by men or women during 1999 were fitness related.

Some sport activities that were popular in 1997 no longer appeared in the top 10 sport activities frequently participated in by men and women. For example, bowling was among the top 10 activities for both men and women in 1997, but was not so for either sex during 1999. Top 10

sports for men in 1997 included billiards (third), baseball (fifth), and golf (sixth).

There was an overall increase in frequent sports participation by women in 1999 compared with 1997. In addition, there was a dramatic increase of female athletes. The number of girls on high school teams increased by 40 percent between 1990 and 1998 according to "U.S. Trends in Team Sports," a report by the SGMA.

Other Sports Trends

The number of people strapping on in-line skates has grown rapidly. In-line skating was the fastest-growing sport from 1987 to 1997—an 849 percent increase— among both males and females. (See Table 5.5.) In-line skating also made women's top 10 sports to participate in frequently during 1999. (See Table 5.4.) A 2000 report from the SGMA said that 32 million Americans participated in in-line skating. Six million of them started in 1998 alone. Two of 10 households had someone who skated in-line.

On the other hand, racquetball lost the greatest share of participants during the 1990s. In 1997, 6.2 million people played racquetball, a 41 percent drop from 1987. (See Table 5.5.) The decline might be due to aging baby boomers switching from this high-impact sport to less strenuous sports. Baseball participation dropped 12 percent over the 10-year period. (See Table 5.6.) Experts attributed that decline to the fact that today's youth are not playing as much casual ball in sandlots and parks. In addition, society increasingly encourages athletes to "special-

TABLE 5.4

Most popular sports for women based on "frequent" participation
(Age 6 and older; in thousands)

Activity	1999
1. Recreational walking (52+ days)	23,806
2. Fitness walking (100+ days)	10,538
3. Stretching (100+ days)	9,651
4. Recreational swimming (52+ days)	9,595
5. Recreational bicycling (52+ days)	7,165
6. Treadmill exercise (100+ days)	5,430
7. Basketball (25+ days)	4,666
8. Free weights: hand weights (100+ days)	4,546
9. Calisthenics (100+ days)	4,379
10. In-line skating (25+ days)	4,275

SOURCE: Sporting Goods Manufacturers Association, North Palm Beach, FL, July 26, 2000

TABLE 5.5

Sports participation trends: individual sports
6 yrs. or older, at least once per year (millions)

	1987	1993	1994	1995	1996	1997	One year 1996-97 Chg.%	`Ten year 1987-97 Chg %
Archery	8.6	8.6	9.2	8.4	8.5	7.5	-11.7	-11.8
Badminton	14.8	1.9	11.8	11.7	10.8	9.6	-11.2	-35.0
Billiards	35.3	40.3	46.9	42.4	44.5	42.2	-5.2	+19.6
Bowling	47.8	49.0	53.1	53.1	52.2	53.3	+2.1	+11.4
Boxing	NA	1.3	1.8	NA	NA	NA	NA	NA
Golf	22.3	24.2	26.6	24.6	23.7	26.3	+11.0	+18.1
Racquetball	10.4	7.4	7.7	6.3	6.8	6.2	-9.8	-40.7
Roller hockey	NA	2.3	3.7	4.2	4.1	4.0	-3.1	+72.1[3]
Roller skating (traditional)	NA	22.2	21.0	18.5	15.3	15.0	-1.8	-37.6[1]
Roller skating (in-line wheels)	NA	12.6	18.8	22.5	27.5	29.1	+5.6	+848.9[1]
Skateboarding	10.9	5.4	6.0	6.2	6.8	8.2	+22.0	-24.3
Street hockey	NA	NA	5.2	4.8	NA	NA	NA	NA
Tennis	21.1	19.3	17.9	18.5	19.0	17.5	-8.1	-17.3
Table tennis	NA	17.7	20.1	19.5	18.2	17.1	-6.1	-14.8[2]

Note: Percentages based on figures rounded to nearest thousand participants.

1 Eight-year change

2 Seven-year change

3 Four-year change

SOURCE: *Sports Participation Trends Report, 1997,* Sporting Goods Manufacturers Association, North Palm Beach, FL, 1998

TABLE 5.6

Sports participation trends: team sports
6 yrs. or older, at least once per year (millions)

	1987	1993	1994	1995	1996	1997	One year 1996-97 Chg.%	Ten year 1987-97 Chg. %
Baseball	15.1	15.6	17.0	16.2	14.7	13.3	-9.7	-12.1
Basketball	35.7	42.1	47.3	46.5	45.6	45.1	-1.0	+26.2
Cheerleading	NA	3.3	3.2	3.2	2.9	NA	NA	NA
Football (touch)	20.3	21.2	23.0	20.0	19.4	18.2	-6.4	-10.5
Football (tackle)	11.7	13.1	13.7	12.2	11.7	12.1	+3.5	+3.6
Soccer	15.4	16.4	18.2	16.8	18.1	18.2	+0.7	+18.4
Softball (fast pitch)	NA	NA	NA	3.5	3.1	3.3	+4.8	-5.7[2]
Softball (slow pitch)	NA	NA	NA	24.5	23.9	20.5	-14.2	-16.5[2]
Softball (total)	31.0	30.1	30.8	26.0	25.3	22.1	-12.6	-28.6
Volleyball (hard surface)	NA	31.7	32.5	28.0	26.4	23.6	-10.8	-27.6[1]
Volleyball (sand/beach)	NA	13.5	14.2	13.3	12.6	10.5	-16.4	+2.3[1]

Note: Percentages based on figures rounded to nearest thousand participants.

[1] Eight-year change

[2] Two-year change

SOURCE: *Sports Participation Trends Report, 1997,* Sporting Goods Manufacturers Association, North Palm Beach, FL, 1998

ize" in a particular sport, rather than playing several, as was once common.

BASKETBALL

Playing basketball is a tremendously popular activity in the United States. Basketball is the second-most popular spectator sport and the most popular participatory team sport. Furthermore, in 1997 in collegiate athletics, basketball (1,916) accounted for more teams than any other sport, including tennis (1,635), cross-country (1,630), soccer (1,372), track (1,137), golf (950), baseball (829), and football (601). (Football, track, and baseball accounted for more individual athletes because of their larger team size, although football and baseball did not report any women's NCAA teams.)

Between 1992 and 1996, the number of female players grew 16 percent, while the number of male players grew 12 percent. (See Figure 5.2.) According to American Sports Data, a slight drop in the number of players since 1994 was a result of a drop in the number of male players. According to Gregg Hartley, executive director of the American Basketball Council, basketball has surpassed volleyball in popularity as a team sport among females. In fact, women's college basketball, once watched by just the parents and friends of the players, is now carried on television and the NCAA playoffs sell out.

According to a report from the SGMA, the overall decline in basketball participation continued in 1998, dropping to 42.4 million. The SMGA suggested that reasons for a drop in participation might be the increased popularity of other activities, such as in-line skating, computers, and video games. In 1999, however, 11.2 million persons said that basketball was their favorite activity, an all-time high, indicating that basketball had a core following of participants. In addition, high school play was on the rise for both boys and girls.

Since 1987 fewer people play basketball at school, while more play at home. In 1996, 27 percent played at a school gym; 23 percent, at home; 11 percent, schoolyards; and the remainder, elsewhere (or no response). (See Figure 5.3.) Nonwhite individuals who lived in major metropolitan areas (21 percent) were slightly more likely to play basketball than the general population (19 percent). In 1996 the average male basketball player had played basketball for 10.5 years; the average female, 6 years.

The American Basketball Council reported that, in 1997, more than 45 million Americans played basketball. A growing proportion were parents playing at home with their children. Gregg Hartley reported that as basketball was gaining popularity on television, adjustable-height basket systems and smaller baskets were created, opening the game to younger players, and helping to make the game a more important family activity. Between 1988 and 1997, wholesale sales of basketball equipment rose 62 percent, from $95 million to $154 million. (See Figure 5.4.) Nevertheless, for the first time since these statistics were compiled, sales of basketballs and basketball equipment declined in 1998 to $150 million.

SOCCER

Increasing numbers of Americans are playing soccer. The *1998 Soccer Participation Survey,* prepared by the Soccer Industry Council of America, found that 18.2 million people played soccer in the previous year, up slightly from 18.1 million in 1996; those who played frequently—25 or more days a year—rose from 7.7 mil-

FIGURE 5.2

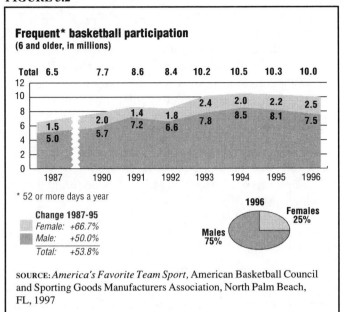

Frequent* basketball participation
(6 and older, in millions)

* 52 or more days a year

Change 1987-95
Female: +66.7%
Male: +50.0%
Total: +53.8%

SOURCE: *America's Favorite Team Sport,* American Basketball Council and Sporting Goods Manufacturers Association, North Palm Beach, FL, 1997

FIGURE 5.4

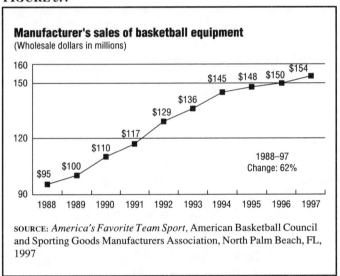

Manufacturer's sales of basketball equipment
(Wholesale dollars in millions)

1988–97
Change: 62%

SOURCE: *America's Favorite Team Sport,* American Basketball Council and Sporting Goods Manufacturers Association, North Palm Beach, FL, 1997

FIGURE 5.3

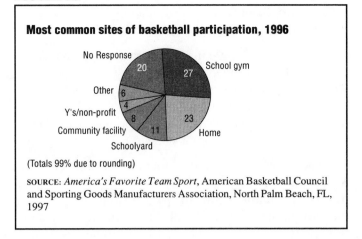

Most common sites of basketball participation, 1996

(Totals 99% due to rounding)

SOURCE: *America's Favorite Team Sport,* American Basketball Council and Sporting Goods Manufacturers Association, North Palm Beach, FL, 1997

TABLE 5.7

Soccer players: a profile

	Key findings	
Total participants (U.S. population 6 yrs. or older, at least once per year)	18,226,000	(100%)
Male	11,081,000	(61%)
Female	7,145,000	(39%)
Under 18	13,627,000	(75%)
18 and over	4,599,000	(25%)
Frequent participants (25 or more days/year)	8,502,000	(47%)
"Core" participants (52 or more days/year)	3,341,000	(18%)
"Aficionados" (soccer is favorite activity)	4,036,000	(22%)

SOURCE: Soccer Industry Council of America, North Palm Beach, FL

lion to 8.5 million. Three-fourths of players were under the age of 18. (See Table 5.7.) Soccer was most popular in Utah (17 percent of residents played), followed by Kansas (14 percent), Iowa (13 percent), Missouri (12 percent), and Minnesota (11 percent). Soccer participation increased 11 percent during the 1990s, with play on high school teams increasing by 65 percent and play on U.S. Youth Soccer Association programs increasing by 76 percent according to "U.S. Trends in Team Sports," a report by the SGMA.

Nevertheless, while huge numbers of young people play soccer, this youthful interest has not translated into adult play. Several attempts at creating professional soccer leagues have failed, and the current Major League Soccer organization continues to struggle. Even the play-ing of the World Cup in Atlanta, Georgia, in 1994 failed to develop any long-term interest.

BOWLING

Bowling ranks as America's most popular participant sport. In 1997, according to American Sports Data, 53.3 million Americans went bowling (see Table 5.5); 8.6 million were "frequent" bowlers (25 or more days per year). According to an SGMA report, however, the number of bowlers declined to 50.6 million in 1998. More alarming for the industry was the steady decline in the number of frequent bowlers—from 11 million in 1987 to 8.5 million in 1998, according to the SGMA.

In an attempt to increase participation during the 1990s, many bowling facilities underwent upgrading and made a successful effort to improve their image. Although the overall number of bowling centers declined, the consolidation of centers resulted in the closing of many antiquated bowling lanes, some of which were then replaced by state-of-the-art facilities with attractive decor, updated scoring and playing equipment, good food service, and other entertainment, in better locations. Some megacenters also provided access to golf driving ranges, basketball, skating, billiards, and even microbreweries.

Other changes were made to attract the youth market. Centers often included "Rock 'n' Bowl" and "Cosmic Bowling," bowling under ultraviolet lights with lanes, pins, and bowlers set aglow. Bowlers aged 12–17 made up 38 percent of America's bowlers according to an SGMA report released in February 2000.

The average household income of bowlers was $48,400, somewhat more than the average of $44,700 for the U.S. population. Bowling participation was growing the most in the West and South, although the North Central region of the United States had the highest participation. Only slightly more males than females bowled. Whites accounted for 76 percent of bowlers; Hispanics, 12 percent; blacks, 9 percent; and other, 3 percent.

BILLIARDS AND POOL—COMING OF AGE

Despite a slight decline in the number of billiard players since 1996, billiards remains a favorite participation sport in the United States. In 1997, 42.2 million Americans played billiards at least once (see Table 5.5), and 9.2 million played frequently (25 days or more). In 1998 the number of billiards players declined to 39.7 million.

More males (65 percent) than females (35 percent) played billiards, although the growth of the numbers of female players (25 percent) has been greater than that of men (17 percent) since 1987. Whites accounted for 74 percent of players; Hispanics, 13 percent; blacks, 9 percent; and other, 4 percent. By location, people in the North Central region accounted for 27 percent of players; the Pacific, 17 percent; the South Atlantic, 16 percent; the South Central, 15 percent; the Mid-Atlantic, 14 percent; the Mountain region, 7 percent; and New England, 4 percent.

The average household income of billiards players in 1997 was $46,000, compared with $44,700 for the general population. The growth rate has been greatest in the 35–54 age group (59 percent), while the only decline was in those over the age of 55 (-12 percent).

Pool halls are no longer limited to dark and dreary backs of bars. Billiard and pool tables are now found in a variety of sites, including multi-activity entertainment centers, which might include video games, basketball hoops, indoor golf, sports bars, and restaurants. Billiards and pool are also springing up in food courts at large military bases and college student centers. Even traditional pool halls have changed; many are better lighted and more "wholesome" in decor. Some do not serve alcohol. These changes have not only increased the availability of billiards and pool, but have made the environment in which they are played more appealing to those who might not try the games otherwise.

TENNIS

Tennis was played in the 1960s primarily among the affluent. The game became "fashionable" in the 1970s, but apparently many tennis players turned to aerobics and other fitness activities in the 1980s. In 1997, 17.5 million Americans played tennis, down 8 percent from 1996 and down 17 percent since 1987. (See Table 5.5.) The average household income of tennis players in 1997 was $55,400, well above the household average of $44,700. Public courts were used by 67 percent of tennis players; private clubs, 32 percent; and apartment complexes, hotels, or home courts by the remaining 1 percent. Slightly more males played tennis than females.

GOLF

According to the U.S. Department of Commerce, public golf courses are one of the leading amusement and recreation growth industries, surpassing sports and recreation clubs, bands, orchestras, entertainers, amusement parks, and physical fitness facilities.

In 1997, 26.3 million Americans played golf, up 11 percent from 1996 and 18 percent from 1987. (See Table 5.5.) Among those over the age of 55, golf was the fourth-favorite sport; for adult men, golf ranked sixth in popularity. Watching golf on television was enjoyed by 5 percent of Americans.

CHAPTER 6

GAMBLING IN AMERICA

Gambling has always been a popular form of recreation in North America. George Washington liked to play cards, and Benjamin Franklin printed and sold playing cards. Americans were so fond of playing cards that when the British Stamp Act put a one-shilling tax on playing cards, people were very upset. The anger people felt about the taxes on playing cards and tea was one of the main causes of the American Revolution. During the colonial period, lotteries (a system of raising money by selling numbered tickets and distributing prizes to the holders of numbers drawn at random) were used to raise money to establish the colony of Virginia. In 1777 the Continental Congress held a $5 million lottery to pay for the Revolutionary War.

By the 1800s Americans were known for their gambling. Visitors to this country said it was impossible to talk to a person from Kentucky without hearing the phrase, "I'll bet you!" Large riverboats that went up and down the Mississippi and Ohio rivers carrying passengers or freight almost always had a casino where gamblers played cards and other games of chance. At the end of the Mississippi River was New Orleans, a city famous for gambling. After the Civil War, adventurers went searching for gold and silver in the West, and virtually every mining town had a few gambling casinos.

Beginning in the 1870s, however, most forms of gambling and all lotteries were outlawed by states, following a scandal in the Louisiana lottery. This state lottery operated nationwide and the scandal involved bribery of state and federal officials. In 1985 Congress forbid shipments of lottery tickets across state lines and in 1990 outlawed the use of the mail for lotteries.

HELPING TO FINANCE THE GROWTH OF THE NATION

Although gambling has always been popular in the United States, many people have opposed it because they believed gambling could be a threat to both individuals and the community. Many people become addicted to gambling, and some lose their homes, families, and careers. Furthermore, during the Prohibition Era (1920–33), when alcohol was outlawed, organized crime moved into the profitable worlds of alcoholic beverages and gambling. Although legal gambling has become acceptable for many, the association with organized crime and corruption still taints the activity in the minds of others.

Lotteries began a revival in 1964 when New Hampshire created a state lottery. New York followed suit in 1966. Between 1970 and 1975, 10 more states established lotteries. In 1999, 37 states and the District of Columbia operated lotteries.

TYPES OF LEGAL GAMBLING

There are five primary forms of legal gambling in the United States: bingo, lotteries, pari-mutuel betting, off-track betting, and casinos. Bingo is the most common form of legalized gambling. Lotteries are allowed in 37 states; Washington, D.C.; Puerto Rico; and the Virgin Islands. Forty-three states, Puerto Rico, and the Virgin Islands permit thoroughbred racing. Twenty-two states and Puerto Rico allow casino gambling. Table 6.1 shows the types of gambling activities available throughout the United States and its jurisdictions. Sports gambling is legal and operating in Montana, Nevada, North Dakota, and Oregon. Almost all the money bet legally on sports is bet in Nevada.

TRENDS IN GAMBLING PARTICIPATION

In 1996 a Gallup poll found that participation in some forms of gambling was up, while the rate for others was down. In 1996, 57 percent of respondents reported they had purchased a lottery ticket, up from just 18 percent in 1982. A far higher percentage of people visited casinos in 1996 (27 percent) than in 1982 (12 percent), and a higher percentage of people played video poker in 1996 (17 percent) than in 1992 (11 percent). (See Table 6.2.)

TABLE 6.1

United States gaming at a glance

	Charitable bingo	Charitable games	Card rooms	Casinos & gaming	Non-casino devices	Indian casinos	Indian bingo	Sports betting	Lottery operated games					Parimutuel wagering							
									Video lottery	Keno-style games	Instant/pulltabs	Lotto games	Numbers games	Greyhound	Jai-alai	Harness	Quarterhorse	Thoroughbred	Inter-track wagering	Off-track wagering	Telephone wagering
Alabama	●						●							●		◆	■	■	●		
Alaska	●	●					●														
Arizona	●	●				●	●				●	●	★	●			●	●	●	●	
Arkansas														●			◆	●	●		
California	●	●	●			●	●			●	●	●	●			●	●	●	●	●	
Colorado	●	●	●	●		●	●		■		●	●		●			●	●	●	●	
Connecticut	●	●				●	●				●	●	●	●	●	◆	◆	◆	●	●	●
Delaware	●	●							●		●	●	●			●	●	●	●		
D.C.	●	●									●	●	●								
Florida	●	●	●			●	●				●	●	●	●	●	●	●	■	●	●	
Georgia	●									●	●	●	●								
Hawaii																					
Idaho	●	●				☆	●				●	●		■			●	●	●		
Illinois	●	●		●							●	●	●			●	●	●	●	●	
Indiana	●	●	●	●							●	●	●			●	◆	●	●	●	
Iowa	●	●		●	●	●	●				●	●	●	●		●	●	●	●	●	
Kansas	●	●				●	●			●	●	●		●		●	■	●	●	●	
Kentucky	●	●									●	●	●			■	●	●	●	●	●
Louisiana	●	●		●	●	●	●				●	●	●	●		■	●	●	●	●	●
Maine	●	●					●				●	●	●			●		■	●	●	
Maryland	●	●	●		●					●	●	●	●			●	●	●	●	●	◆
Massachusetts	●	●								●	●	●	●	●		●	■	●	●	●	
Michigan	●	●		★		●	●			●	●	●	●			●	●	●	●	●	
Minnesota	●	●	◆			●	●				●	●				●	●	●	●	●	
Mississippi	●	●		●		●	●				●	●				●	●	●	●		
Missouri	●	●		●						●	●	●	●			■	■	■	◆	◆	
Montana	●	●	●	▼	●		●	●			●	●				◆		■	●	●	
Nebraska	●	●				▲	●			●	●	●				●	■	●	●		
Nevada	●	●	●	●	●	●	●	●						■	■	■	●			●	●
New Hampshire	●	●									●	●	●	●		●		●	●	●	
New Jersey	●	●	●	●							●	●	●			●		●	●	●	
New Mexico	●	●		●	★	●	●				●	●				●	●	●	●	●	
New York	●	●				●	●			●	●	●	●			●	■	●	●	●	
North Carolina	●	●		▼		●	●									●	●	●	●		
North Dakota	●	●	●			●	●	●			●	●				■	●	●	●		
Ohio	●	●								●	●	●				●	●	●	●	◆	●
Oklahoma	●	●				☆	●				●	●				◆	●	●	●	●	
Oregon	●	●	●			●	●	●	●		●	●	●			●	●	●	●	●	★
Pennsylvania	●	●									■	●				●	●	●	●		●
Rhode Island	●	●				●			●	●	●	●		●	●	■		■	●		
South Carolina	●				●																
South Dakota	●	●	●	●		●	●		●		●	●				■		●	■	●	
Tennessee	●															◆	◆	◆	◆	◆	◆
Texas	●	●					●				●	●	●	●			●	●	●	●	
Utah																	○				
Vermont	●	●									●	●	●	■		■		■	◆		
Virginia	●	●									●	●	●			●	●	●	●		
Washington	●	●	●	▲		▲	●			●	●	●				■	●	●	●		
West Virginia	●	●					●	●	●	●	●	●		●		◆	■	●	●		
Wisconsin	●	●				●	●				●	●	●	●		◆	◆	◆	●		
Wyoming	●	●				●					●					◆	●	●			
Puerto Rico	●			●								●	●					●	●	●	
Virgin Islands				◆								●							●	●	

● *Legal and operative*
★ *Implemented since June 1998*
▲ *Table games only (no slots)*

◆ *Authorized but not yet implemented*
▼ *Commercial bingo, keno, or pulltabs only*
■ *Permitted by law and previously operative*

○ *Operative but no parimutuel wagering*
□ *Previously operative but now not permitted*
☆ *Compacts signed for non-casino gambling, such as parimutuel wagering and lotteries; however, casino games may be operating*

SOURCE: "*International Gaming and Wagering Business*," August 1998. Supplement, BPA International, New York, NY, 1998

Recreation

TABLE 6.2

Types of gambling in last year — trends

(Those saying "yes")

Please tell me whether or not you have done any of the following things in the past 12 months. First, how about: played bingo for money; visited a casino; bet on a horse race; bought a state lottery ticket; bet on a professional sports event such as baseball, basketball, or football; bet on a college sports event such as basketball or football, bet on a boxing match; participated in an office pool on the world series, super-bowl, or other game; gambled for money on the internet; played a video poker machine; done any other kind of gambling not mentioned here.

Lottery ticket	
1996 Jun 27-30	57%
1992	56
1989	54
1982†	18
Visited casino	
1996 Jun 27-30	27%
1992	22
1989	21
1984	18
1982†	12
Office pool	
1996 Jun 27-30	23%
Video poker	
1996 Jun 27-30	17%
1992	11
Pro sports	
1996 Jun 27-30	10%
1992	12
1989	22
1984	17
1982†	15
Played bingo	
1996 Jun 27-30	9%
1992	9
1989	13
1982†	9
1950	12
College sports	
1996 Jun 27-30	7%
1992	6
1989	14
Horse race	
1996 Jun 27-30	6%
1992	12
1989	14
1984	11
1982†	9
1950	4
1938	10
Boxing match	
1996 Jun 27-30	3%
1992	6
1989	8
Gambled on internet	
1996 Jun 27-30	1%
Other	
1996 Jun 27-30	10%

† Gallup for *Gaming Business Magazine*

SOURCE: *The Gallup Poll Monthly*, The Gallup Organization, Princeton, NJ, July 1996

Betting on sports events, however, was generally down. In 1996, 10 percent of respondents bet on pro sports, down significantly from 22 percent in 1989. College sports were gambled on by 7 percent, compared with 14 percent in 1989. Only 3 percent bet on boxing events in 1996, down sharply from 8 percent in 1989. Horse racing had been gambled on by 6 percent, compared with 14

percent in 1989. Participation in office pool betting was admitted by 23 percent, and 1 percent reported gambling on the Internet. (See Table 6.2.)

Gallup took another look at gambling in 1999. (See Table 6.3.) Lottery ticket purchases had stayed at the same levels as 1996, but there were increases in almost all other areas, compared with 1996 figures. Casino gambling had increased to 31 percent from 27 percent. Video poker had increased to 20 percent from 17 percent. And betting on professional sports events had increased to 13 percent from 10 percent.

The 1999 survey also separated responses according to annual income. Interestingly, in almost all categories of gambling, middle- to upper-income households had the highest participation in gambling. Collectively, households with $25,000 or more in annual income were more likely (75 percent) to have gambled than households with less than $25,000 (61 percent). Gallup also found that men were somewhat more likely to have gambled during the past year (77 percent) compared with women (62 percent). Persons with a high school degree or higher education were more likely to have gambled (71–72 percent) than persons with less education (61 percent).

International Gaming and Wagering Business reported in August 1998 that 10 cents of every dollar consumers spent on leisure was spent on commercial games. In 1997 gamblers spent $51 billion on such games, out of $496 billion spent on leisure goods, services, and activities. (See Figure 6.1.)

WHERE AMERICANS GAMBLE THEIR MONEY

In 1998 Americans bet $677.4 billion on legal gambling in the United States, up from $635.8 billion in 1997. Almost three-fourths of that was wagered in casinos—mostly in Las Vegas, Nevada; or Atlantic City, New Jersey—and on riverboats. Most of the remainder was bet at games on Indian reservations (nearly 15 percent) or lotteries (7 percent). (See Table 6.4.)

International Gaming and Wagering Business reported in August 1998 that gamblers spent an average of 3.9 hours per day gambling in Las Vegas, down from 5 hours per day in 1991 and 1994.

BINGO AND OTHER CHARITABLE GAMES

Charitable gambling is permitted in all states except Arkansas, Hawaii, Tennessee, and Utah. It constitutes 5–6 percent of the total amount wagered on legalized gambling in the United States. Of that total, bingo accounts for approximately half. Charity games include bingo, raffles, casino nights, "pull tabs," lucky 7s, pickle cards, and jar tickets. Bingo sessions are a common form of fundraising by charitable organizations, such as churches, synagogues, or service clubs. It is a relatively inexpensive

TABLE 6.3

Please tell me whether or not you have done any of the following things in the past 12 months:

"Yes, have done" (%)	Total	Under $25K	$25–44.9K	$45–74.9K	$75K+
Bought a state lottery ticket	57%	53%	61%	65%	56%
Gambled at a casino	31	23	34	37	37
Participated in an office pool	25	13	27	35	36
Played a video poker machine	20	17	20	23	22
Bet on a professional sports event	13	9	15	15	16
Played bingo for money	11	10	12	10	8
Participated in riverboat gambling	10	6	12	12	13
Bet on a horse race or dog race	9	5	12	9	14
Bet on a college sports event	9	5	11	11	12
Gambled for money on the Internet	*	*	*	*	1

SOURCE: *The Gallup Poll Monthly,* The Gallup Organization, Princeton, NJ, July 8, 1999

FIGURE 6.1

The U.S. leisure economy, 1997
(Total $495.5 billion)

SOURCE: *International Gaming & Wagering Business,* August 1998 Supplement, BPA International, New York, NY, 1998

way for people to do something together socially. Industry experts believe that bingo has peaked in popularity and revenues. (See Figure 6.2.) Non-bingo charitable gambling has, however, been growing. (See Figure 6.3.)

PARI-MUTUEL WAGERING

Pari-mutuel wagering combines wagers into a common pool. Sports in which pari-mutuel wagering takes place are horse racing, greyhound racing, and jai alai. Winners are paid according to odds calculated with reference to the amounts bet on each contestant.

Horse Racing

The largest sector in pari-mutuel wagering is horse racing. Horse racing has a long history in America. The first American horse race took place in New York in the late 1660s. Several larger tracks, such as Churchill Downs, in Louisville, Kentucky, have been in operation since the 1800s.

Many Americans enjoy going to the racetrack for entertainment, some to enjoy the beautiful animals, many more to gamble. Horse racing is a popular spectator sport, although it has declined significantly in popularity relative to other forms of gambling. About 43 million people visited the track in 1996 (see Table 6.5), a huge drop (61 percent) from the more than 63.8 million people who attended horse-racing events in 1990, but more than the 39 million in 1995. Daily average attendance dropped from 4,610 persons per track in 1990 to 2,940 persons per track in 1995, then rebounded to 3,481 persons in 1996.

The amounts wagered, however, have gone up. Although there are 150 racetracks in America, most betting takes place elsewhere. Satellite broadcasting makes it possible to simultaneously broadcast races between racetracks or at off-track betting sites where there are no races. In addition, at-home pari-mutuel betting is now possible and several companies provide 24-hour racing channels. There is even an Internet simulcast. It has been estimated that off-track and simulcast betting, permitted in 38 states, now account for 77 percent of pari-mutuel wagering.

Account wagering also is possible in nine states. Patrons are permitted to set up accounts at racetracks and, in eight of those states, can phone in their bets from anywhere. According to the *National Gambling Impact Study Commission Report,* issued in June 1999, about $550 million was bet using account wagering during 1998. Pari-mutuel wagering on horse races is legal in 43 states and generates about $3.25 billion in gross revenue according to the *National Gambling Impact Study Commission Report.*

There are three major forms of horse racing: thoroughbred, harness, and quarter horse. In the United States, thoroughbred is, by far, the most popular form of

TABLE 6.4

Trends in gross wagering (handle), 1982–98
(dollars in millions)

	1982 Gross Wagering (Handle)	1997 Gross Wagering (Handle)(Revised)	1998 Gross Wagering (Handle)	1982-1998 Increase/(Decrease) In Gross Wagering (Handle)		Average Annual Rate 1982-1998
				Dollars	Percent	
Pari-mutuels						
Horses						
On-Track	$9,990,600	$3,603,200	$3,481,400	($6,509,200)	-65.15%	-(6.38%)
ITW		6,115,000	6,320,400	6,320,370	N/A	N/A
OTB	1,707,300	5,620,400	5,870,400	4,163,140	243.85%	8.02%
Total	11,697,900	15,338,600	15,672,200	3,974,310	33.97%	1.84%
Greyhounds						
On-Track	2,208,600	1,306,500	1,236,900	(971,680)	-44.00%	-(3.56%)
ITW		797,300	820,800	820,780	N/A	N/A
OTB		147,400	146,500	146,490	N/A	0.54(1)
Total	2,208,600	2,251,100	2,204,100	(4,400)	-0.20%	-0.01%
Jai Alai	622,800	212,600	198,400	(424,350)	-68.14%	-6.90%
Total pari-mutuels	**14,529,200**	**17,802,400**	**18,074,800**	**3,545,550**	**24.40%**	**1.37%**
Lotteries						
Video lotteries		11,862,200	14,181,600	14,181,590	N/A	N/A
Other games	4,088,300	34,341,700	34,350,200	30,261,910	740.21%	4.23%
Total lotteries	**4,088,300**	**46,103,900**	**48,531,800**	**44,443,500**	**1087.09%**	**16.72%**
Casinos						
Nevada/NJ Slot Machines	14,400,000	133,895,200	137,519,100	123,119,060	854.99%	15.15%
Nevada/NJ Table Games	87,000,000	189,250,400	181,757,200	94,757,230	108.92%	4.71%
Deepwater Cruise Ships		3,437,700	3,692,100	3,692,090	N/A	N/A
Cruises-to-nowhere		3,093,000	3,884,500	3,884,510	N/A	N/A
Riverboats		115,817,800	135,505,700	135,505,730	N/A	N/A
Other Land-Based Casinos		7,932,900	7,982,600	7,982,570	N/A	N/A
Other Commercial Gambling		451,800	466,800	466,780	N/A	N/A
Non-Casino Devices		16,188,700	17,089,900	17,089,940	N/A	N/A
Total casinos	**101,400,000**	**470,067,400**	**487,897,900**	**386,497,900**	**381.16%**	**10.32%**
Legal bookmaking						
Sports books	415,200	2,431,400	2,269,100	1,853,900	446.55%	11.20%
Horse books	122,800	141,500	137,000	14,190	11.56%	0.69%
Total bookmaking	**538,000**	**2,572,900**	**2,406,100**	**1,868,090**	**347.25%**	**9.81%**
Card rooms	1,000,000	10,423,600	11,007,300	10,007,350	1000.73%	16.17%
Charitable bingo	3,000,000	3,910,400	3,972,900	972,920	32.43%	1.77%
Charitable games	1,200,000	6,034,100	6,172,900	4,972,860	414.40%	10.78%
Indian reservations						
Class II		2,997,200	3,180,800	3,180,770	N/A	N/A
Class III		78,934,300	96,174,900	96,174,900	N/A	N/A
Total Indian reservations		**81,931,500**	**99,355,700**	**99,355,670**	**N/A**	**N/A**
Internet gambling		N/A	N/A	N/A	N/A	N/A
Grand total	**$125,755,500**	**$638,846,100**	**$677,419,300**	**$551,663,800**	**438.68%**	**11.10%**

Note: Lottery handles for 1982 are for the twelve months ending June 30th
Columns may not add to totals due to rounding.

SOURCE: Eugene Martin Christiansen, "Steady Growth for Gaming," *International Gaming & Wagering Business*, vol. 20, no. 8, August 1999.

horse racing, followed by harness and then quarter horse racing. The horse racing industry is a big business, responsible for creating an estimated 119,000 jobs.

Greyhound Racing—The Sport of Queens

Once a favorite pastime of Queen Elizabeth I of England, dog racing became known as the "Sport of Queens." Originally, a hare would be released and a pair of grey-

hounds set in pursuit. In the early 1900s, a mechanical lure replaced the hare, eliminating the killing of a rabbit.

The first American greyhound racetrack opened in Emeryville, California, in 1919. At the start of 2001, there were 49 tracks operating in 15 states, but dog racing is in a decline. Many tracks have closed due to low attendance. During 1996, 15,151 races took place, down from 16,110 races in 1995. About 28 percent of races were held in Flori-

FIGURE 6.2

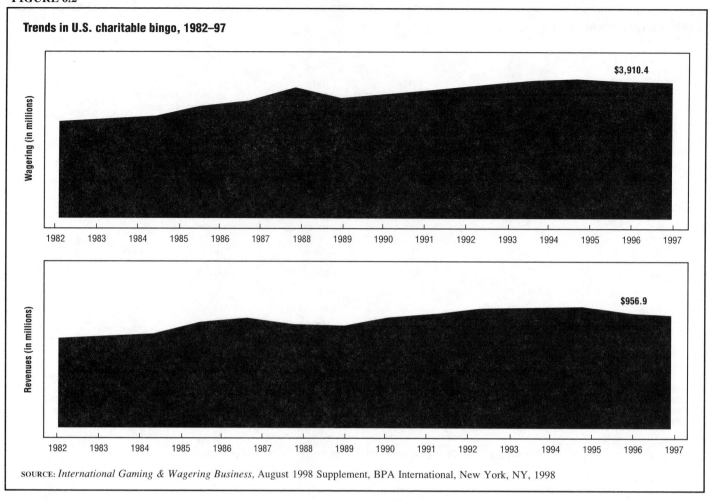

Trends in U.S. charitable bingo, 1982–97

Wagering (in millions)

$3,910.4

1982 1983 1984 1985 1986 1987 1988 1989 1990 1991 1992 1993 1994 1995 1996 1997

Revenues (in millions)

$956.9

1982 1983 1984 1985 1986 1987 1988 1989 1990 1991 1992 1993 1994 1995 1996 1997

SOURCE: *International Gaming & Wagering Business,* August 1998 Supplement, BPA International, New York, NY, 1998

da. (See Table 6.6.) Almost 31 million people attended dog-racing events in 1991; by 1996, only 16 million went.

Like horse tracks, dog tracks have turned to simulcasting and off-track betting. The total amount wagered on greyhounds in 1996 was $2.3 billion, generating revenues of $505 million and creating 30,000 jobs.

The animal rights movement has protested the sport, claiming the dogs are mistreated. Although the claims led many track owners to improve the conditions, activists have persuaded some legislators to ban racing or rescind existing permits. The declining financial condition of many tracks is, however, the primary reason that numerous tracks have closed.

Jai Alai

Jai alai is a fast-paced game in which the players, using a large curved basket strapped to their arms, whip a small ball made of goatskin against the three walls and floor of a huge playing court (fronton). Jai alai was invented in the seventeenth century in Spain and France. Although the game is popular in Latin America, its popularity has been declining in the United States. At the start of 2001, it was legal in only three states—Florida, Rhode Island, and Connecticut.

The popularity of jai alai peaked during the 1980s when more than $600 million was bet annually. By 1996 the amount bet had fallen below $240 million. During 1996 there were 2,542 jai alai events, down from 3,619 in 1990. Approximately 2.3 million people attended, an average of 1,774 people per meet. (See Table 6.7.)

Florida once had 10 frontons. It now has only 6. The future of the sport in the United States is uncertain. Cruises, many of which offer casino gambling, and lotteries have taken considerable money from the frontons. Most jai alai frontons now offer simulcasting of horse races, which gamblers can bet on.

Problems for Pari-mutuels

Because of the increased availability of other forms of gambling, pari-mutuels are facing hard times. Off-track betting and simulcasting has helped (at the beginning of the twenty-first century, 38 states permitted interstate simulcast betting), but many owners of racetracks and frontons say more is needed to stay competitive. Track owners want to install electronic gambling devices (EGDs) as an additional source of revenue. (EGDs are discussed below.) As of 2001, Delaware, Rhode Island, South Carolina, and West Virginia permitted EGDs at

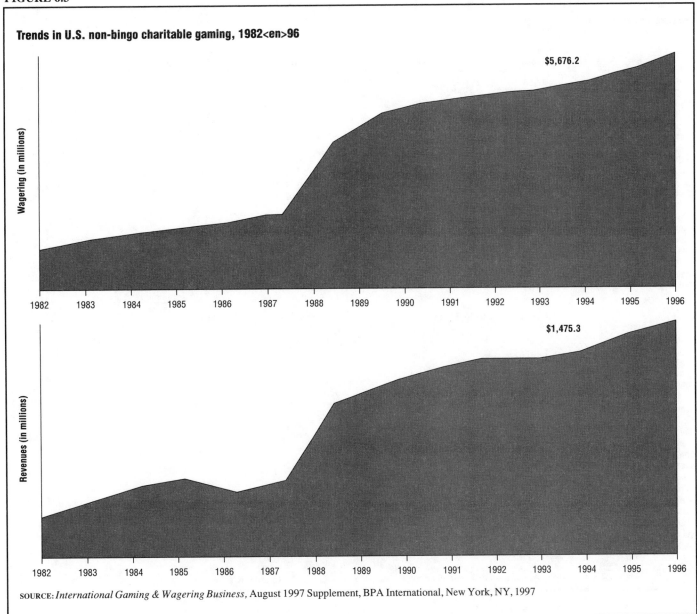

FIGURE 6.3

Trends in U.S. non-bingo charitable gaming, 1982<en>96

$5,676.2

$1,475.3

SOURCE: *International Gaming & Wagering Business,* August 1997 Supplement, BPA International, New York, NY, 1997

racetracks. This is a highly controversial issue. According to the National Coalition Against Legalized Gambling, attempts to legalize EGDs at racetracks have been defeated in 12 states since 1995.

LOTTERIES

A lottery is a game in which people purchase numbered tickets in hopes of winning a prize. A person wins if the number on his or her ticket is the one drawn from a pool of all the tickets purchased for that event. In the case of instant lotteries, a bettor wins if the ticket contains a predetermined winning number. Raffles are a form of lottery in which the prize is usually goods rather than cash.

Lotteries are created and run by government. In 1999, 37 states and the District of Columbia had operating lotteries. Lottery revenues may go into the general fund of

the state or may be earmarked for particular purposes, such as education, parks, or police pension funds. Developments in technology and communications have created many possible ways to conduct lotteries. There are five principal types of lottery games:

- Instant games, in which the player scratches off the ticket to find out whether and what he or she has won

- Daily numbers games, in which players can pick a combination of numbers

- Lotto, or a variation of it, in which numbers are chosen from a large set of possibilities with winners selected periodically. Powerball is a popular lottery of this type

- Video keno, in which the player chooses numbers with drawings held very frequently (sometimes several times an hour)

TABLE 6.5

Live meeting attendance

	Thoroughbred	Quarter horse	Harness	Mixed	Total
Alabama					
Arizona				598,552	598,552
Arkansas	791,891				791,891
California	8,985,187	881,573	745,916	1,081,655	11,694,331
Colorado				261,166	261,166
Connecticut					
Delaware	411,996		130,963		542,959
Florida	1,714,263		383,181		2,097,444
Idaho				160,084	160,084
Illinois	1,626,401		912,748		2,539,149
Indiana	65,750		103,099		168,849
Iowa				N/A	N/A
Kansas				32,543	32,543
Kentucky	1,754,004		92,083		1,846,087
Louisana	602,342	31,744			634,086
Maine			N/A		N/A
Maryland	2,157,668		395,503		2,553,171
Massachusetts	903,523		180,956		1,084,479
Michigan	410,000		772,274	8,488	1,190,762
Minnesota			806	322,805	323,611
Montana				N/A	N/A
Nebraska	239,598				239,598
Nevada				N/A	N/A
New Hampshire	253,732		N/A		253,732
New Jersey	1,404,059		1,529,330		2,933,389
New Mexico				533,303	533,303
New York	2,585,480		1,426,775		4,012,255
North Dakota				5,000	5,000
Ohio	1,334,461	6,395	1,542,726		2,882,582
Oklahoma	492,846			373,120	865,966
Oregon				N/A	N/A
Pennsylvania	2,105,882		542,734		2,648,616
Rhode Island					
South Dakota				N/A	N/A
Texas	575,367	237,784		147,718	960,869
Vermont			N/A		N/A
Virginia					
Washington	865,198			51,037	916,235
West Virgina	595,841				595,841
Wisconsin					
Wyoming				N/A	N/A
Totals	**29,875,489**	**1,157,496**	**8,758,094**	**3,575,471**	**43,366,550**

SOURCE: *Pari-Mutuel Racing—1996*, Association of Racing Commisioners International, Inc., Lexington, KY

- Electronic gambling devices (EGDs). These allow bettors to play a game, such as video poker, and receive an immediate payout. EGDs are discussed in more detail below

As more and more states have introduced lotteries to raise money for government, people have had the opportunity to do more gambling. State lottery tickets are sold in grocery stores, convenience stores, gas stations, and many other places. When the winnings become unusually large, or two or three states get together for a big lottery jackpot, the lines to buy lottery tickets can be long. According to the August 1999 *International Gaming and Wagering Business* magazine, in 1998 Americans bet $48.5 billion on lotteries. (See Table 6.4.) Per capita sales grew from $35 per capita in 1973 to $150 in 1997. (See Figure 6.4.)

In general, poor people play lottery games less frequently than middle and high income groups. The lottery appeals to young people more than to older persons. Most people who played the game reported playing it regularly.

Electronic Gambling Devices

Electronic gambling devices (EGDs) include stand-alone slot machines, video poker, video keno, and other types of gambling games. Because EGDs are portable, they make gambling possible at locations that are not, like racetracks or casinos, dedicated to the business of gambling. EGDs are becoming popular in bars, truck stops, convenience stores, and other locations that were formerly not places to gamble. Some states, such as Louisiana, Montana, and South Carolina, permit private business to operate EGDs. In other states, such as Oregon and California, EGDs are operated by the state lottery.

In addition to legal EGDs, in other states there are lots of illegal EGDs, or "gray machines," so called

TABLE 6.6

Greyhound racing

	Number of live performances	Number of live races	Attendance			
			Live racing	Average	ITW	QTW
Bimingham, AL	464	6,042	761,159	1,640	Included in Live	
Greene County, AL	306	3,978	N/A			
Macon County, AL	507	6,591	535,787	1,057		
Mobile County, AL	462	5,737	303,592	657		
Alabama total	1,739	22,348	N/A	N/A		
Arizona	771	10,869	412,901	536		473,712
Arkansas	413	5,668	773,000	1,872		
Colorado	601	11,597	1,094,223	1,821		
Connecticut	744	10,363	415,621	559		
Florida	4,358	60,095	5,691,843	1,306		
Idaho	No live greyhound racing					
Iowa	523	7,589	N/A			
Kansas	735	10,470	677,382	922		
Massachusetts	1,018	N/A	1,345,856	1,322		
New Hampshire	826	12,071	423,991	513		
Oregon	121	1,574	N/A			
Rhode Island	363	5,445	N/A			
South Dakota	No live greyhound racing					
Texas	907	10,884	1,235,407	1,362		
West Virginia	728	10,973	997,971	1,371		
Wisconsin	1,304	N/A	1,300,673	997		
Totals	**15,151**	**N/A**	**N/A**	**N/A**		**473,712**

Note: Number of races in Bimingham, Greene County, Iowa, Rhode Island, and Texas are estimated.

SOURCE: *Pari-Mutuel Racing—1996*, Association of Racing Commisioners International, Inc., Lexington, KY

FIGURE 6.4

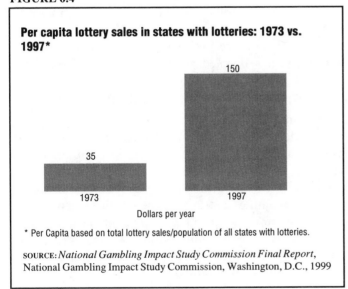

Per capita lottery sales in states with lotteries: 1973 vs. 1997*

Dollars per year

* Per Capita based on total lottery sales/population of all states with lotteries.

SOURCE: *National Gambling Impact Study Commission Final Report*, National Gambling Impact Study Commission, Washington, D.C., 1999

because they exist in a gray area of the law. Basically, if such a machine is used for amusement and no proceeds are paid out, then gambling laws have not been broken. Nevertheless, according to the 1999 *National Gambling Impact Study Commission Report,* establishments with such machines surreptitiously pay winners. Gray machines are common in bars and fraternal organizations in many states. It has been estimated that there are 15,000–30,000 gray machines in West Virginia; 10,000 each in New Jersey and Alabama; and as many as 65,000 in Illinois.

Opponents of EGDs say that it is too easy to become addicted to them. They are easily accessible and provide immediate and intense gambling experiences that can be continued for a long time.

CASINO GAMBLING

Technically, a casino is any room or rooms in which gaming is conducted. When most Americans think of casinos, they picture hotel/gambling/entertainment complexes such as those in Las Vegas or Atlantic City. Before 1990 only Nevada and Atlantic City permitted casinos. In 2001 casinos were legal in 28 states and came in various forms. In addition to the Las Vegas resort-type casinos, there were nearly 100 riverboat casinos in six states and about 260 casinos on Indian reservations. Nevada had 429 full-scale casinos and nearly 2,000 slots-only casinos.

Casino games include slot machines and table games, such as keno, bingo, twenty-one, craps, roulette, baccarat, and poker. In 1998 Americans bet $487.9 billion on casino games.

Who Are Casino Visitors?

With the increased availability of casino gambling, more people are visiting casinos. The national *Harrah's Survey of U.S. Casino Gaming Entertainment 1997* (Memphis, Tennessee) reported that, in 1996, 32 percent of U.S.

TABLE 6.7

Jai-alai events

	Number of performances	Number of games	Live meet attendance	Average attendance	Live handle ($)	Inter-track off-track handle ($)
Connecticut	448	6,466	311,657	696	52,743,008	26,986,531
Florida	1,909	25,475	2,057,264	1,078	153,473,661	35,934,039
Rhode Island	185	2,405	N/A		4,273,506	
Totals	2,542	34,346	N/A	N/A	210,490,175	62,920,570

	Total handle ($)	Total takeout ($)	Effective takeout rate	Total government revenue ($)	Pari-mutuel tax revenue ($)	Breakage to gov't ($)
Connecticut	79,729,539	15,887,536	19.9%	2,464,951	2,095,515	81,065
Florida	189,407,700	44,645,557	23.57%	9,273,222	7,470,934	
Rhode Island	4,273,506	880,862	20.61%	196,826	170,940	2,539
Totals	273,410,745	61,393,955	22.45%	11,934,999	9,737,389	83,604

	Uncashed tickets to gov't ($)	Fronton license revneue ($)	Occupational license revenue ($)	Admission tax to gov't ($)	Miscellaneous government revenue ($)	Effective parimutuel tax rate
Connecticut	198,400		10,290	78,566	1,115	2.73%
Florida	514,716	990,120	56,720	224,847	15,885	3.94%
Rhode Island	20,119		3,228			4.06%
Totals	733,235	990,120	70,238	303,413	17,000	3.59%

SOURCE: *Pari-Mutuel Racing—1996*, Association of Racing Commisioners International, Inc., Lexington, KY

households had gambled at a casino during the previous year, up dramatically from 17 percent in 1990. (See Figure 6.5.) These people made an estimated 176 million trips to casinos. Much of the increase was attributable to the new casino locations. While 70 million trips were made to either Nevada or Atlantic City, 106 million were made to the new casino destinations. (See Figure 6.6.)

The study found that because of the increased availability of the casinos, the number of trips made by each household that frequented casinos rose from 2.7 per year in 1990 to 4.8 in 1996. Not surprisingly, the top 10 states that provided the most visitors were the states located nearest Nevada and New Jersey, states near riverboat gaming casinos, and Wisconsin and Minnesota, which have the largest number of Indian casinos. (See Figure 6.7.) The profile of the typical gambling household did not differ much from the average household, although they tended to earn somewhat more. (See Figure 6.8.)

Riverboat and Cruise Gambling

Some people gamble on riverboats (either seaworthy excursion boats or stationary barges) or on cruises. Riverboat casinos are relatively new, having begun in Iowa in 1991. By 1997 revenues from riverboat gambling totaled $6.1 billion.

Although the cruise lines emphasize that gambling is just one of many attractions to be enjoyed on their cruises, virtually all major cruise lines provide gambling. Many of the cruises, however, have a limit of $100–200 to control losses. "Cruises to nowhere" or "day trips" are gambling opportunities available at coastal ports in Florida, Texas, New York, and Georgia. The ships travel 3–12 miles into international waters, where neither state nor federal gambling laws apply. Since 1985 the day-cruise gambling industry has more than doubled, growing from 10 to 25 vessels.

Casino Gambling on American Indian Reservations

The Indian Gaming Act of 1988 (PL 100-497) permitted American Indian tribes to introduce gambling on their reservations. By 1996 one could visit 281 gambling facilities belonging to 184 tribes across the United States. (See Figure 6.9.) By 1998 there were 298 Indian gambling facilities operating in 30 states. The revenue has provided employment for American Indians and monies for investment in housing, education, health care, and other reservation needs. Tribal gaming revenue increased from $212 million in 1988 to $6.7 billion in 1997. (See Figure 6.10.)

Two-thirds of American Indian tribes, however, do not participate in gambling at all. Only 146 of the 554 tribes of American Indians participated in gambling. In addition, the 20-largest American Indian gambling facilities accounted for more than half of all revenues. Some Indian casinos were operating at a loss and a few had to shut down due to financial loss.

Generation Xers—Customers of the Future

By 2000, 57 million Americans in their twenties and early thirties—Generation Xers—accounted for 21 per-

FIGURE 6.5

Casino penetration* among U.S. households, 1990–96

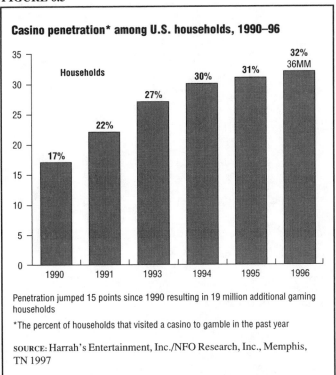

Penetration jumped 15 points since 1990 resulting in 19 million additional gaming households

*The percent of households that visited a casino to gamble in the past year

SOURCE: Harrah's Entertainment, Inc./NFO Research, Inc., Memphis, TN 1997

FIGURE 6.6

Visits to U.S. casino destinations, 1990–96

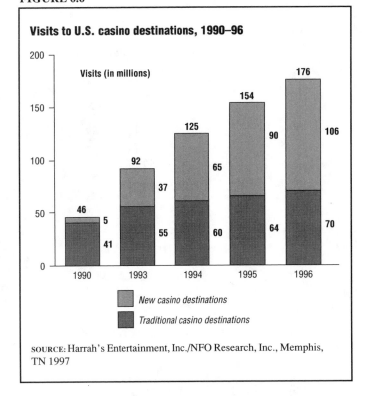

SOURCE: Harrah's Entertainment, Inc./NFO Research, Inc., Memphis, TN 1997

FIGURE 6.7

Top 10 casino feeder states, 1996

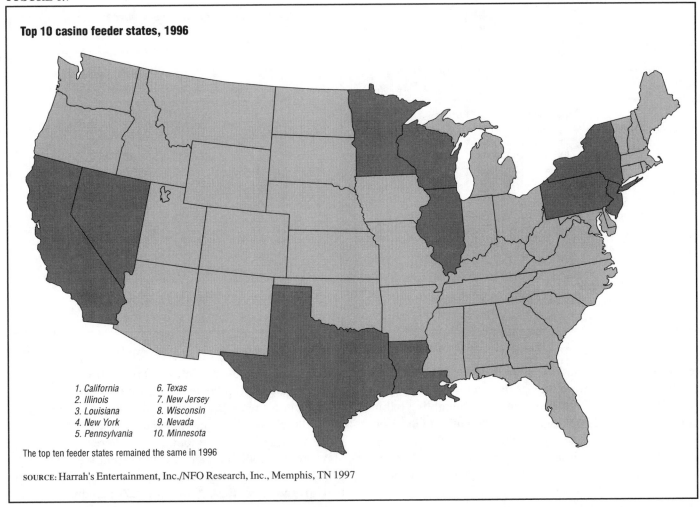

1. California
2. Illinois
3. Louisiana
4. New York
5. Pennsylvania
6. Texas
7. New Jersey
8. Wisconsin
9. Nevada
10. Minnesota

The top ten feeder states remained the same in 1996

SOURCE: Harrah's Entertainment, Inc./NFO Research, Inc., Memphis, TN 1997

FIGURE 6.8

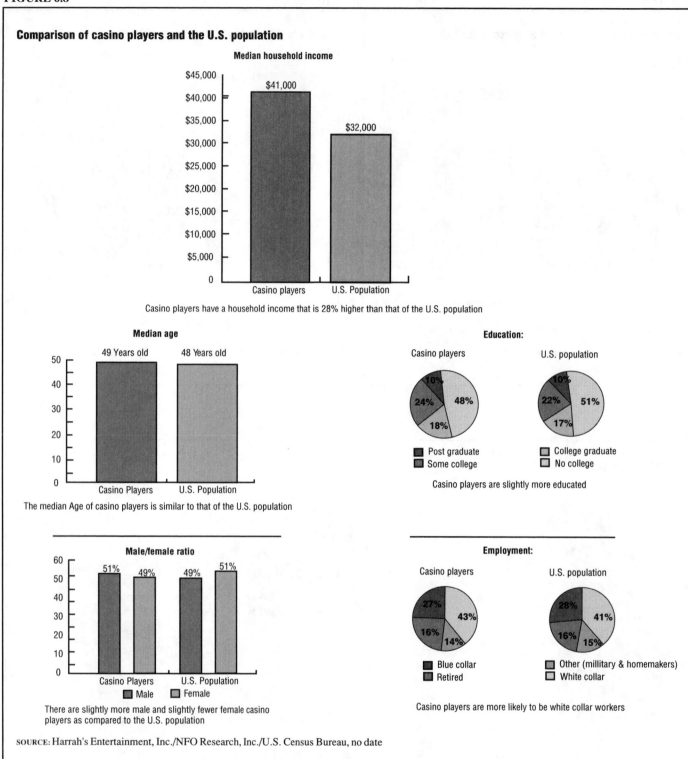

Comparison of casino players and the U.S. population

SOURCE: Harrah's Entertainment, Inc./NFO Research, Inc./U.S. Census Bureau, no date

cent of the U.S. population. As they age, their preferences and habits will greatly influence the gambling industry. In 1997 JB Research Company studied the gambling habits of the group and concluded that 55 percent of Gen Xers visited casinos in the past year, compared with 32 percent of all households. When those young people become established in their careers and affluent, they will become the gaming industry's new market.

Of those surveyed, almost 70 percent were students and single, and 20 percent were professionals. Although their incomes were below those of national gamblers in general (because they were not full-time workers and they were younger), educational levels were significantly above those of all gamblers. Sixty percent were currently in college, 31 percent had been graduated, and 9 percent had advanced degrees. Nationally, 28 percent of casino

FIGURE 6.9

Distribution of Indian gaming facilities

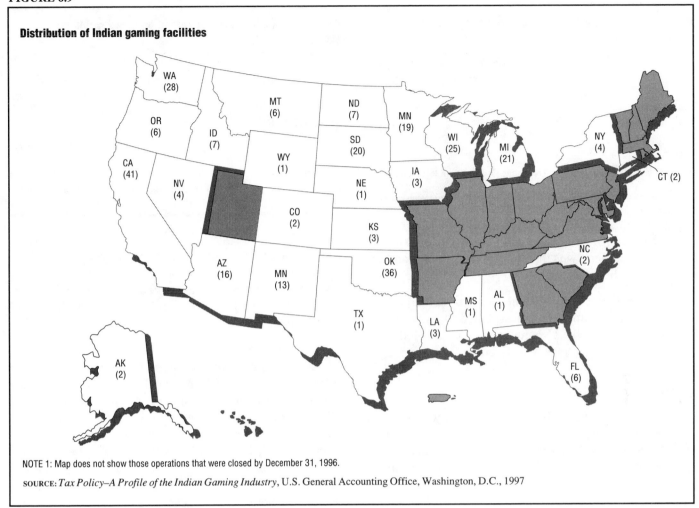

NOTE 1: Map does not show those operations that were closed by December 31, 1996.

SOURCE: *Tax Policy–A Profile of the Indian Gaming Industry*, U.S. General Accounting Office, Washington, D.C., 1997

players had four-year degrees, and 10 percent had advanced degrees. Among the general population of gamblers, 22 percent had college or advanced degrees.

Of the respondents, 94 percent preferred Las Vegas. Las Vegas was mentioned 20 percent of the time, followed by Indian casinos at 18 percent, Reno at 14 percent, Laughlin (Nevada) at 11 percent, and cruise ships at 7 percent.

The average annual gambling budget for Generation Xers was $123.77, less than the $172 per person for the population at large. Most respondents (62 percent) spent less than $100; 7 percent spent more than $400. Although Generation Xers do not have the resources to spend as much today, they will likely in the future.

Other activities enjoyed by Generation Xers while on casinos trips included bars (61 percent), shopping (48 percent), nightclubs (39 percent), movies (26 percent), and game arcades (20 percent). Females placed shopping high on the list—70 percent of them enjoyed shopping, while only 27 percent of men did. More than one-third of females went to the movies while on a gambling trip, compared with only 19 percent of men. Although both

FIGURE 6.10

Increase in tribal gambling revenues: 1988 vs. 1997

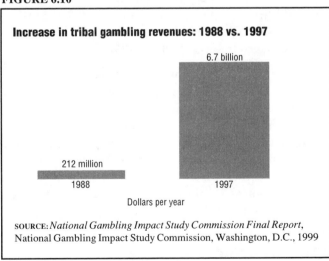

SOURCE: *National Gambling Impact Study Commission Final Report*, National Gambling Impact Study Commission, Washington, D.C., 1999

groups enjoyed bars and nightclubs, neither were major supporters of game arcades (18 percent of females and 21 percent of males).

There was considerable difference between male and female preferences in casino games. Females were more

TABLE 6.8

Do you sometimes gamble more than you think you should?

	Gamble too much? - trend		
	Apr 1989	Nov 1992	Jun 1996
Yes	10%	9%	7%
No/doesn't apply (vol.)	90	91	93
No opinion	0	0	*
	100%	100%	100%

*Less than 0.5%

SOURCE: *The Gallup Poll Monthly,* The Gallup Organization, Princeton, NJ, July 1996

TABLE 6.9

Has gambling ever been a source of problems within your family?

	Create family problems? - trend		
	Apr 1989	Nov 1992	Jun 1996
Yes	4	5	5
No/doesn't apply (vol.)	96	94	95
No opinion	*	1	*
	100%	100%	100%

*Less than 0.5%

SOURCE: *The Gallup Poll Monthly,* The Gallup Organization, Princeton, NJ, July 1996

likely to choose slot machines (84 percent) than males (53 percent). Blackjack was the preference of males and the number-two choice for women.

Females had a smaller gambling budget than males. Almost half the women spent less than $50; only 26 percent of men did. Fully 21 percent of men gambled more than $300 annually, versus only 4 percent of women.

SPORTS GAMBLING

People can bet legally on sports in only two states. Nevada has 142 legal sports books that permit wagering on professional and amateur sports. Oregon has a game associated with the Oregon lottery that permits betting on pro football games.

Almost all the money wagered legally on sporting events such as football and basketball games is bet in Nevada. Championship games, such as the Super Bowl or the World Series, are some of the most popular sporting events on which people bet. Sport bets totaling $2.3 billion were placed in Nevada during 1998.

In addition, an unknown number of people participate in illegal gambling, such as office or social "pots" on sports events. Estimates of illegal sport betting range from $80 billion to $380 billion annually. In addition, some Americans cross the Mexican border to gamble or travel to the Caribbean or Central America, where sports gambling is legal. In 1982 police arrested 41,200 people for illegal gambling; by 1997 the number had fallen to just 15,900.

INTERNET GAMBLING

Internet gambling first appeared on the World Wide Web in the summer of 1995. By May 1998, according to the *National Gambling Impact Study Commission Report* of 1999, there were 90 online casinos, 39 lotteries, 8 bingos, and 53 sports books. A year later that had increased to 250 online casinos, 64 lotteries, 20 bingo games, and 139 sports books. Sebastian Sinclair, a gambling industry

analyst for Christiansen/Cummings Associates, estimated that Internet gambling revenues increased from $300 million in 1997 to $651 million in 1998. Another study found estimated growth from $445 million to $919 million during the same period.

Gambling experts contend that there are two major obstacles to the growth of Internet gaming—the Federal Wire Act, which makes it illegal to use interstate telephone lines to gamble, and the proposed Internet Gambling Prohibition Act that would criminalize both the operator and customer of an Internet gaming facility. Many countries, as well as the U.S. Department of Justice, are concerned about the enforceability of an Internet gambling prohibition. Most Internet gambling businesses operate offshore and are licensed by foreign governments.

Several states have passed or are considering laws prohibiting Internet gambling. Some attorneys general have brought lawsuits against Internet gambling businesses. The Department of Justice has arrested or caused arrest warrants to be issued for 22 Internet gambling operators. Several persons have been indicted.

Nevertheless, Internet gambling is growing. The *International Gaming and Wagering Business* estimated that by 2001, 19 million Americans would be gambling on the Internet. A report issued in 2000 estimated that there were 700 Web sites offering gambling in the form of sports betting or casino-style games. Projections of revenue from Internet gambling vary widely, but one study predicted revenues of $1.5 billion in 2000 and $3 billion or more by 2002.

FOR SOME PEOPLE, RECREATION BECOMES ADDICTION

Although gambling is a form of recreation and fun for many people, for some, gambling is a compulsion or addiction. This behavior may cause them to gamble away their paychecks and go deeply into debt. It may harm marriages and other relationships with children, other relatives, and friends.

In 1996 a Gallup poll reported that when respondents were asked if they had ever gambled more than they should, 7 percent, down from 9 percent in 1992, reported that they had done so. (See Table 6.8.) When asked whether gambling had ever been a problem within their family, 5 percent said it had, the same as in 1992. (See Table 6.9.) When asked if they ever went back to win lost money, 16 percent said they did some of the time, and 1 percent every time.

Gambling more than they intended to was admitted to by 23 percent of the respondents. Men (28 percent) were more likely than women (18 percent) and younger people more likely than older people to have gambled more than they intended. About 5 percent said they would like to stop gambling but could not. About 3 percent of those interviewed saw gambling as a way to escape their problems.

A 1997 study by the Harvard Medical School Division on Addictions estimated that 7.5 million Americans had gambling problems. Of those 7.5 million, 2.2 million were estimated to have pathological problems with gambling.

CHAPTER 7
VACATIONS AND TRAVEL

Millions of Americans love to vacation and vacation destinations vary from a trip to a national park for camping, fishing, boating, or hiking, to a theme park, such as Disneyland. A vacation can also be a flight to Egypt, a cruise to the Virgin Islands, a romantic three-day weekend, or staying home to read a book. The way Americans vacation and travel and what they expect from their vacation time have been changing as U.S. society has evolved. Most people believe that travel and vacationing improve the quality of their lives.

DOMESTIC TRAVEL

Where Do Americans Travel?

The U.S. Department of Transportation periodically conducts the *American Travel Survey,* which collects information about trips of 100 miles or more taken by American household members. Its latest survey (1995) reported that Americans took nearly 685 million long-distance trips in 1995. About 96 percent of those trips—656 million trips, totaling 1 billion person trips (a person trip is one person traveling on a trip, 50 miles or more, one-way, away from home; for example, if three people from the same household go together on a trip, the trip is counted as one household trip and three person trips)—were to destinations in the United States. Only 4 percent of trips were outside the United States. Approximately 55 percent of trips were to locations outside the traveler's home state (interstate). (See Table 7.1 for selected characteristics of domestic travelers.)

The South was the destination in 38 percent of all trips. The South Atlantic division of the South accounted for one of five (19.6 percent) of all person trips. The East North Central division of the Midwest attracted the next largest number of travelers, approximately 15 percent, and the Pacific division in the West drew over 13 percent. Less than 5 percent of trips were to locations in the New England division of the Northeast. (See Figure 7.1.)

According to data collected by the Travel Industry Association of America (TIA), the total miles traveled by U.S. citizens increased from 968 million in 1994 to over 1 billion in 1999. The most miles of travel in 1999 occurred in July (12 percent), June (10 percent), and August (10 percent), followed by November, December, and May, each with 9 percent. Travel figures for November and December likely reflect holiday travel. Travel in summer months is more likely because school generally is not in session during those months, allowing families to take children on vacations.

Means of Travel

The *American Travel Survey* found that three of four trips within the United States in 1995 were taken in a personal vehicle, resulting in over 280 billion vehicle miles of travel on U.S. highways. Personal vehicles were the favorite means of travel for shorter trips. (See Figure 7.2.) Travelers used commercial air travel for 19 percent of all trips; 72 percent of those trips were 1,000 miles or more, round-trip, with a median distance of 1,732 miles. Tour or charter buses were used for only 2 percent of trips. Intercity bus and train travel accounted for less than 1 percent of trips. Intercity bus and train trips were more likely to be taken by persons 65 and over, females, minorities, those less educated, and those living in households with income under $25,000.

Two-thirds of trips by personal vehicle were for pleasure; only 19 percent were for business. Of commercial air travel, 43 percent was for business, while 47 percent was for pleasure. Most trips by charter or tour bus, ship, boat, or ferry were for leisure.

The TIA reported that air travel grew at a faster rate than auto travel from 1995 through 1999.

Reasons for Travel

The TIA reported that Americans took 1.01 billion person trips in 1999. Two-thirds of the trips in 1999 were for

TABLE 7.1

Travel in the United States by selected characteristics: 1995

(Trips of 100 miles or more, one way. U.S. destinations only. Data based on a sample and subject to sampling variability)

Trip characteristic	Household trips Number (thous.)	Per-cent	Person trips Number (thous.)	Per-cent	Person miles Number (mil.)	Per-cent	Personal use vehicle trips Number (thous.)	Per-cent	Personal use vehicle miles Number (mil.)	Per-cent
Total	**656,462**	**100.0**	**1,001,319**	**100.0**	**826,804**	**100.0**	**505,154**	**100.0**	**280,127**	**100.0**
Principal means of transportation:										
Personal use vehicle	505,154	77.0	813,858	81.3	451,590	54.6	505,154	100.0	280,127	100.0
Airplane	129,164	19.7	161,165	16.1	355,286	43.0	NA	NA	NA	NA
Commercial airplane	124,884	19.0	155,936	15.6	347,934	42.1	NA	NA	NA	NA
Bus	17,340	2.6	20,445	2.0	13,309	1.6	NA	NA	NA	NA
Intercity bus	2,755	0.4	3,244	0.3	2,723	0.3	NA	NA	NA	NA
Charter or tour bus	11,890	1.8	14,247	1.4	9,363	1.1	NA	NA	NA	NA
Train	4,200	0.6	4,994	0.5	4,356	0.5	NA	NA	NA	NA
Ship, boat, or ferry	391	0.1	614	0.1	1,834	0.2	NA	NA	NA	NA
Other	213	—	243	—	429	0.1	NA	NA	NA	NA
Round trip distance:										
Less than 300 miles	194,098	29.6	306,433	30.6	74,658	9.0	185,418	36.7	45,159	16.1
300 to 499 miles	174,389	26.6	274,045	27.4	106,007	12.8	159,743	31.6	61,779	22.1
500 to 999 miles	140,046	21.3	214,006	21.4	146,631	17.7	106,846	21.2	72,114	25.7
1000 to 1999 miles	76,110	11.6	108,331	10.8	153,316	18.5	36,722	7.3	49,953	17.8
2000 miles or more	71,819	10.9	98,503	9.8	346,192	41.9	16,425	3.3	51,123	18.3
Mean (miles)	872	NA	827	NA	NA	NA	555	NA	NA	NA
Median (miles)	438	NA	425	NA	NA	NA	368	NA	NA	NA
Calendar quarter:										
1st quarter	130,963	19.9	200,331	20.0	155,603	18.8	99,549	19.7	50,801	18.1
2nd quarter	168,669	25.7	258,400	25.8	208,266	25.2	130,135	25.8	72,421	25.9
3rd quarter	193,913	29.5	304,542	30.4	261,463	31.6	152,862	30.3	90,558	32.3
4th quarter	162,917	24.8	238,047	23.8	201,471	24.4	122,607	24.3	66,346	23.7
Main purpose of trip:										
Business	192,537	29.3	224,835	22.5	212,189	25.7	125,036	24.8	61,929	22.1
Pleasure	372,586	56.8	630,110	62.9	506,971	61.3	305,571	60.5	177,698	63.4
Visit friends or relatives	195,468	29.8	330,755	33.0	264,769	32.0	159,981	31.7	92,190	32.9
Leisure*	177,119	27.0	299,355	29.9	242,201	29.3	145,590	28.8	85,508	30.5
Rest or relaxation	65,017	9.9	115,154	11.5	100,838	12.2	53,780	10.6	33,598	12.0
Sightseeing	24,272	3.7	42,649	4.3	50,781	6.1	18,069	3.6	14,654	5.2
Outdoor recreation	39,899	6.1	65,418	6.5	41,620	5.0	35,987	7.1	19,407	6.9
Entertainment	37,456	5.7	58,757	5.9	42,929	5.2	27,920	5.5	14,531	5.2
Personal business	91,319	13.9	146,338	14.6	107,621	13.0	74,532	14.8	40,490	14.5
Other	19	—	36	—	23	—	16	—	9	—
Vacation or weekend trips:										
Vacation trip	301,197	45.9	515,383	51.5	484,144	58.6	236,055	46.7	154,167	55.0
Weekend trip	270,231	41.2	441,385	44.1	325,864	39.4	216,743	42.9	118,290	42.2
1 or 2 nights away from home	151,377	23.1	252,581	25.2	132,782	16.1	133,147	26.4	60,906	21.7
3 to 5 nights away from home	118,854	18.1	188,804	18.9	193,083	23.4	83,597	16.5	57,384	20.5
Travel party type and size:										
One adult, no children under 18	386,479	58.9	386,510	38.6	352,350	42.6	275,034	54.4	144,795	51.7
Two or more adults, no children under 18	155,148	23.6	299,485	29.9	248,762	30.1	133,163	26.4	79,273	28.3
One adult, 1 or more children under 18	29,436	4.5	67,959	6.8	48,083	5.8	24,879	4.9	13,827	4.9
Two or more adults, 1 or more children under 18	66,086	10.1	225,875	22.6	158,334	19.2	60,497	12.0	34,758	12.4
No adult, 1 or more children under 18	19,313	2.9	21,489	2.1	19,275	2.3	11,581	2.3	7,472	2.7
Mean travel party size (household members)	1.6	NA	2.2	NA	NA	NA	1.7	NA	NA	NA
Nights away from home:										
None	164,032	25.0	239,727	23.9	104,444	12.6	140,914	27.9	49,619	17.7
1 to 3 nights	321,227	48.9	502,465	50.2	331,504	40.1	259,354	51.3	131,559	47.0
4 to 7 nights	121,279	18.5	184,766	18.5	243,546	29.5	76,380	15.1	61,317	21.9
8 or more nights	49,924	7.6	74,361	7.4	147,309	17.8	28,506	5.6	37,631	13.4
Mean excluding none (nights)	4.5	NA	4.3	NA	NA	NA	4.0	NA	NA	NA
Type of lodging at destination:										
One or more nights at destination	486,305	100.0	751,958	100.0	709,097	100.0	359,745	100.0	226,001	100.0
Friend's or relative's home	211,832	43.6	345,506	45.9	290,428	41.0	170,271	47.3	103,180	45.7
Hotel, motel, or resort	201,264	41.4	282,929	37.6	318,323	44.9	126,160	35.1	82,447	36.5
Rented cabin, condo, or vacation home	17,607	3.6	30,648	4.1	31,161	4.4	14,631	4.1	10,809	4.8
Owned cabin, condo, or vacation home	20,205	4.2	38,572	5.1	26,269	3.7	18,103	5.0	9,819	4.3
Camper, trailer, recreational vehicle, tent	11,944	2.5	22,208	3.0	15,836	2.2	11,663	3.2	8,204	3.6
Other type of lodging	23,452	4.8	32,095	4.3	27,080	3.8	18,917	5.3	11,542	5.1
Nights at destination:										
Mean nights at destination	4.2	NA	4.0	NA	NA	NA	3.8	NA	NA	NA
Friend's or relative' home	4.3	NA	4.0	NA	NA	NA	3.6	NA	NA	NA
Hotel, motel, or resort	3.0	NA	3.0	NA	NA	NA	2.8	NA	NA	NA

— Represents zero or a value too small to report.   * Includes other leisure purposes not shown separately.   NA Not applicable.

Note: Numbers and percents may not add to totals due to rounding.

SOURCE: *1995 American Travel Survey*, U.S. Bureau of Transportation Statistics, Washinton, D.C., 1997

FIGURE 7.1

Destinations of person trips by census region and division: 1995
(in thousands)

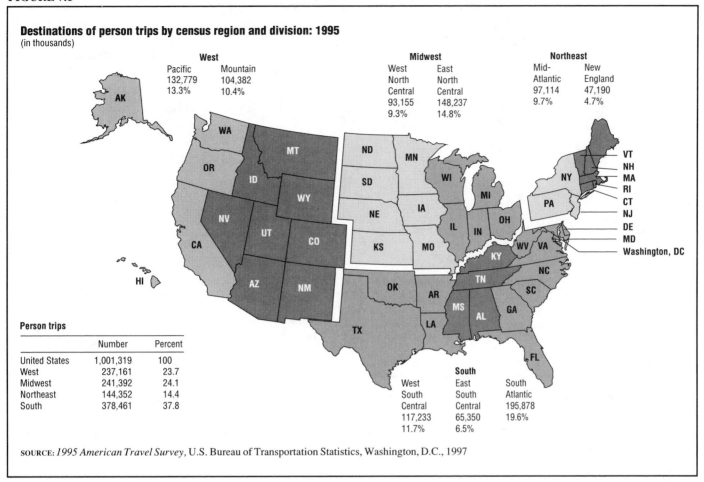

	West		Midwest		Northeast	
	Pacific	Mountain	West North Central	East North Central	Mid-Atlantic	New England
	132,779	104,382	93,155	148,237	97,114	47,190
	13.3%	10.4%	9.3%	14.8%	9.7%	4.7%

Person trips

	Number	Percent
United States	1,001,319	100
West	237,161	23.7
Midwest	241,392	24.1
Northeast	144,352	14.4
South	378,461	37.8

South

West South Central	East South Central	South Atlantic
117,233	65,350	195,878
11.7%	6.5%	19.6%

SOURCE: *1995 American Travel Survey*, U.S. Bureau of Transportation Statistics, Washington, D.C., 1997

---

pleasure. (See Table 7.2.) Of the remaining trips, 17 percent were for business, 4 percent combined business and pleasure, and 13 percent were for personal or other reasons.

The TIA also reported that shopping was the favorite activity of travelers during 1999. (See Figure 7.3.) Thirty-three percent of travelers shopped during a trip. Other popular trip activities included spending time outdoors (17 percent), visiting historical sites or museums (14 percent), going to the beach (10 percent), attending cultural events/festivals (10 percent), and visiting national and state parks (10 percent). Other trip activities engaged in by less than 10 percent of travelers were visiting theme or amusement parks (8 percent), nightlife/dancing (7 percent), gambling (7 percent), attending sporting events (6 percent), and golf/tennis/skiing (4 percent).

Two out of five U.S. adults (38 percent, or 75.3 million) attended an organized sports event, competition, or tournament either as a spectator or participant while traveling in the years 1994 through 1998. Most (70 percent) of these travelers took their most recent trip in 1998. The most popular organized sports events were baseball and softball, with 17 percent of adults traveling 50 miles or more to see or participate in a game between 1994 and 1998. The next

FIGURE 7.2

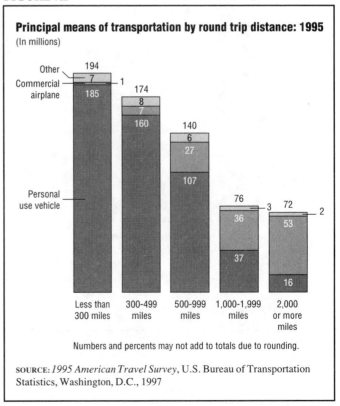

Principal means of transportation by round trip distance: 1995
(In millions)

Numbers and percents may not add to totals due to rounding.

SOURCE: *1995 American Travel Survey*, U.S. Bureau of Transportation Statistics, Washington, D.C., 1997

TABLE 7.2

Total person trips, 1999

Purpose of trip	
Pleasure	66%
Business	17%
Combined business/pleasure	4%
Personal/other	13%
Modes of transportation used	
Auto, truck, RV	76%
Airplane	18%
Bus	2%
Train/ship/other	4%
Top activities for domestic travelers	
Shopping	First
Outdoor activities	Second
Visiting museums and/or historic sites	Third

Note: A person trip is one person traveling 50 miles (one way) or more away from home and/or overnight.
A trip is one or more persons from the same household traveling together.

SOURCE: Travel Association of America; Travelscope, Washington, D.C., no date

FIGURE 7.4

Person trips by purpose and type of lodging: 1995
(In millions)

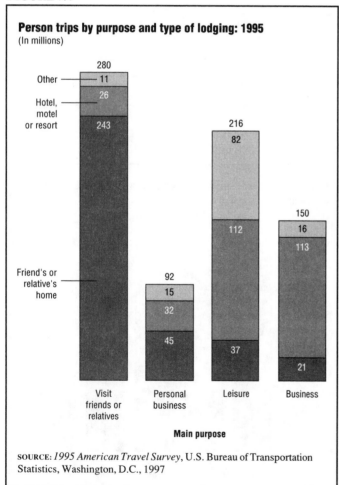

SOURCE: *1995 American Travel Survey*, U.S. Bureau of Transportation Statistics, Washington, D.C., 1997

FIGURE 7.3

Activities participated in by U.S. resident travelers, 1998–99

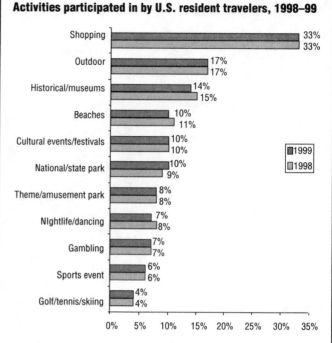

Base = Total respondents (trips of 50 miles or more, one-way, away from home and/or overnight)

SOURCE: Travel Association of America; Travelscope, Washington, D.C. no date

FIGURE 7.5

Travel by age group comparison: 1999
Number of trips (millions)

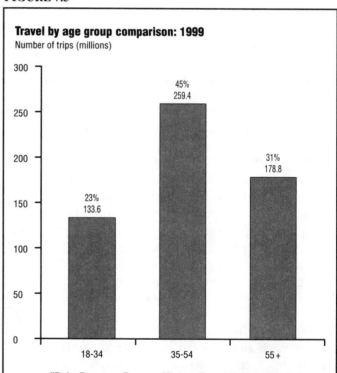

SOURCE: "Baby Boomers Generate Highest Travel Volume in U.S.," *TIA Travel Poll*, Travel Industry Association of America, Washington, D.C., July 7, 2000

TABLE 7.3

Travel with children, 1987–97
(based on trips)

	1987	1988	1989	1990	1991	1992	1993	1994	1995	1996	1997	87–97 change
Total (millions)	567.3	584.9	592.2	589.4	592.4	650.7	648.2	665.3	669.7	682.8	715.9	
% with children	17%	17%	16%	16%	15%	14%	14%	17%	19%	20%	21%	
Trips w/children	96.4	99.4	94.8	106.1	88.9	91.1	90.7	113.1	127.4	136.5	148.8	54%
Pleasure (millions)	348.6	366.7	368.3	361.1	364.3	411.7	413.4	434.3	413.0	432.5	443.2	
% with children	21%	21%	19%	23%	20%	17%	18%	22%	25%	23%	25%	
Trips w/children	73.2	74.9	68.1	83.1	72.9	70.0	74.4	95.5	103.8	100.7	109.1	49%
Business (millions)	185.0	182.8	199.3	182.8	176.9	210.8	210.4	193.2	207.8	192.8	207.4	
% with children	4%	5%	5%	5%	4%	6%	6%	7%	7%	12%	12%	
Trips w/children	7.4	9.1	9.9	9.1	7.1	12.6	12.6	12.7	15.4	23.8	24.4	230%

SOURCE: Travel Industry Association of America, Washington, D.C., 1998

most popular events were football (15 percent), basketball (9 percent), and auto/truck racing (8 percent).

Though usually not a primary (7 percent) or even secondary (9 percent) reason for a trip, about 40 million Americans visited a botanical garden, went on a garden tour, or participated in some garden-related activity while on a trip of 100 miles or more away from home from 1994 to 1998. Ten million did so during 1998. Garden travelers were more likely to be female, married, better educated, older, and had higher incomes than the average American traveler.

Weekend Travel

The growing number of two-career families often makes it difficult for families to schedule long trips. Weekend trips—and "three-day weekends"—have become the practical, if not desirable, solution for such couples.

According to the *American Travel Survey,* weekend travel accounted for 25 percent of all trips in 1995. When a weekend trip is defined as one to five nights that include a Friday and/or Saturday night, the survey found that 44 percent of all travel would be considered weekend trips. For weekend trips of one or two nights, 41 percent were to visit friends or family, 32 percent were for leisure, 13 percent were for business, and 12.5 percent were for personal business. Travelers used personal vehicles for 91 percent of one- or two-night weekend trips. About 7 percent of weekend travel was by commercial air.

Weekend trips have increased dramatically. The TIA reported that weekend trips by Americans increased by 70 percent during the 1990s. Weekend trips now account for more than half of all U.S. travel.

Type of Lodging

Of travelers who spent one or more nights away from home, 47 percent stayed with friends or family, while 38 percent stayed in a hotel or motel. Of travelers who went to visit friends or relatives, 87 percent stayed in the homes of friends or relatives, while three-fourths of business travelers stayed in a hotel or motel. (See Figure 7.4.)

Of those travelers whose main purpose was leisure, 52 percent stayed in a hotel or motel; 23 percent, in cabins or condominiums; 17 percent, with friends or relatives; and 8 percent, in a camper, trailer, or recreational vehicle.

Who Travels?

The TIA reported that baby boomers (35- to 54-year-olds) generated the highest volume of travel in 1999. This age group accounted for 259 million trips (45 percent), more than any other age group. (See Figure 7.5.) Boomers were more likely than other age groups to stay in a hotel (60 percent), travel for business (35 percent), and fly (25 percent). They also spent more on non-transportation items during their trips.

Persons 55 or older accounted for 31 percent of trips, and persons aged 18–34 accounted for 23 percent of trips. (See Figure 7.5.) Forty-four million persons took business trips during 1998. Two of five travelers in 1998 lived alone.

The average annual household income of travelers increased from $50,700 in 1994 to $61,500 in 1999. Almost half of travelers owned cellular phones and more than two-thirds owned computers.

TAKING THE KIDS ALONG. According to the TIA, 21 percent of adults—149 million—said they included a child or children on a trip of 100 or more miles in 1997. That was up from 17 percent of traveling adults who included a child in 1987 and 14 percent in 1993. (See Table 7.3.) Of these travelers, 76 percent took their own child/children on their trips; 16 percent, grandchildren; 8 percent, a niece or nephew; and 6 percent, children from another household.

The 1997 *Better Homes and Gardens Family Vacation Travel Report* found that family travel accounted for 74 percent of all vacation travel in the United States. Children were included on half the family vacations, and 88 percent of all families with children traveled with them.

Children's programs are popular with families. Nearly 60 percent of family travelers used children's services, such as "kids' meals" (41 percent), hotel discounts (30 percent), video and other games (22 percent), supervised activities (13 percent), and baby-sitting (6 percent).

THE NATURE TRAIL

National parks are one of America's biggest tourist attractions. The United States has set aside 80 million acres of land for national parks. The National Park System (NPS) includes parks, monuments, historical and military areas, parkways, recreation areas, nature preserves, rivers, seashores, and lakes. National parks offer many things for families to enjoy doing together or individually, and because visitors' fees are low, a trip to a national park is a popular summer vacation choice for many families with children of all ages. (For more information on national parks, see Chapter 3.)

The TIA reported that nearly 30 million American adults (20 percent of travelers or 15 percent of all U.S. adults) visited a national park in 1998. Residents of the Rocky Mountain region of the United States were most likely to visit a national park, with 37 percent saying they included a national park while traveling. A large share (70 percent) included outdoor activities—hiking (53 percent), camping (33 percent), and fishing (19 percent)—while visiting national parks.

HOT SPOTS—SUMMER VACATIONS

People flock to the beach in the summer. The TIA reported, in 1998, that nearly 50 million travelers claimed that they visited the beaches in June, July, and August. Thirty-five percent—48.8 million adults—traveled 100 miles or more to a beach during the summer. The beach was most popular among men, those with children in the home, and travelers aged 18–34. In the United States, the top destinations for summer travel were the beaches of Florida and California. Of beachgoers, 45 percent stayed overnight in a hotel or motel and 29 percent stayed with family or friends.

ADVENTURE VACATIONING AND TRAVEL

The TIA, in its 1992–97 study, *The Adventure Travel Report, 1997,* reported that one-half of American adults (98 million) had taken an adventure vacation in that period. About 46 percent took "soft adventure" vacations. One in eight (12 percent) vacationers participated in soft vacations that involved wildlife or natural resources, such as animal viewing or bird-watching; 12 percent rode horses; 8 percent toured wilderness areas in off-road vehicles; 4 percent went on safaris to take photographs; and 3 percent visited a cattle or dude ranch. Some facilities began to offer vacation weeks worldwide for those who wanted to ride horseback in rustic settings or learn to ride a motorcycle.

Sixteen percent of American vacationers took "hard adventure" vacations. Among those that involved wildlife or natural resources, 8 percent went whitewater rafting or kayaking; 6 percent, snorkeling or scuba diving; 5 percent, mountain biking; 4 percent, backpacking across wild terrain; 4 percent, mountain climbing; and 3 percent, spelunking (cave exploring). Spouses were the most popular companions for soft adventure, while friends most often accompanied hard adventure vacationers. Hard adventure vacationers spent an average of $465 per trip, while soft adventure travelers spent $325.

People who enjoyed adventurous vacations were most likely to live in the West (19 percent), while 14 percent came from the Midwest. Of men, 20 percent had taken an adventure trip, compared with 12 percent of women. A person was more likely to participate in hard adventures when young. Twenty-two percent of people aged 18–34 and 18 percent of those 35–54 took a hard adventure vacation, compared with only 5 percent of those older than 55.

GOING ON CRUISES—NEW PORTS AND OPTIONS

A New Generation of Cruisers

For many travelers, few experiences can compare to sailing to exotic destinations on a cruise ship. According to the Cruise Lines International Association (CLIA), an organization of 23 member cruise lines, since 1979, when 1.4 million Americans took cruises, the cruise industry has grown 8 percent each year. The CLIA said that through the third quarter of 2000, passenger growth was nearly 16 percent. Cruise ships increased the number of their berths (a place for a ship to dock or anchor) by 11 percent during 2000. The CLIA predicted that when the final figures were in, 6.9 million vacationers would have cruised on U.S. cruise lines that year.

Historically, most cruise passengers were over the age of 60. Today's cruise vacationers are younger, active, and adventurous. More than 44 percent of people who cruised were first-timers. Eight of ten of them reported they would cruise again. The CLIA reported that current cruisers were:

- Spread among all age ranges. The median age was 50 years. Twenty-seven percent were under 40 years, 45 percent were 40–59, and 28 percent were over the age of 60

- Almost equally male (46 percent) and female (54 percent)

- Predominantly married (73 percent), although one in four was single

- Less likely than the average vacationer to have children under 18 in the family

- Spread among all income ranges, with a median income of $58,800. One in five earned less than $40,000 a year

According to the CLIA, cruises sailed, in general, at 91 percent of capacity. In 1997 the average length of cruises was 6.5 days. Cruises averaged a cost of $175 per day per adult, including meals and entertainment. Children often traveled free or at reduced cost. Growth was predicted in all types of cruises, especially short cruises (one to five days).

Unprecedented Cruise Options

Short cruises are extremely popular, with many Americans favoring a long weekend getaway. More than a third of those who cruised took short cruises. Among the most popular destinations for short cruises were the Bahamas, the Caribbean, the west coast of Mexico, the Mediterranean, the Mississippi River, Hawaii, Canada/New England, the West Coast, and Bermuda. Transatlantic crossings and party cruises were also available in shorter trips. Theme cruises included "big band" cruises, arts and crafts, wine and food festivals with famous chefs, Civil War trips, and jazz and film festivals. Many people enjoyed day trips, which often included gambling.

CLIA-member lines visit 1,800 ports of call around the world. From Antarctica to the Caribbean, from Africa to the Mississippi, cruises reach virtually all waters of the world. One can visit ancient Buddhist temples in Indonesia, sip cappuccino in Venice, watch whales on the Pacific Coast, scuba dive in the Caribbean, or shop in Turkey. Other people enjoy just lounging in a deck chair or reading. Cruise ship cuisine is legendary, as is the pampering most cruisers experience.

Also now found on many ships are extensive youth facilities and programs that include kids-only shore excursions. The CLIA reported that 14 percent of people going on cruises traveled with children. Cruise lines such as Disney's Big Red Boat were geared specifically for families.

ECOTOURISM

"Green" (advantageous to the environment) travel is important to many travelers. The TIA reported that 83 percent of travelers supported green travel companies and claimed they were willing to spend an average of 6.2 percent more for travel services and products provided by environmentally responsible travel suppliers.

In the 1990s a large number of ecotourism companies sprang up, promoting vacations that claimed to conserve the environment and directly benefit local people. While some operators succeeded in these goals, others might have used the "eco" label as a marketing device for tours that exposed fragile regions, such as the Amazon River, to tourism without regard for their preservation.

CULTURAL AND HERITAGE TOURISM

Heritage tourism seeks to draw visitors to historic and cultural sites. Although historic and cultural destinations are not as popular with leisure travelers as cities, visits to friends and family, beaches, and lakes, a significant number of travelers choose educational experiences.

According to a 1998 TIA study commissioned by Partners in Tourism, a collaboration of eight national associations and four federal agencies, more than 92.4 million U.S. adults—46 percent of U.S. travelers—included a visit to a historic site on their vacation in the preceding year. Visits to historic sites (31 percent) led the list of favored destinations, followed by museums (24 percent), art galleries (15 percent), live theater (14 percent), festivals (13 percent), and opera (7 percent). Also enjoyed were dance performances (5 percent), film festivals (3 percent), and poetry/literary readings (2 percent). The study also found that the travelers who included a cultural/historic activity while on a trip were more likely than those who did not to:

- Add extra time to their trip because of that activity (29 percent). Part of a day was added by 61 percent; one night by 30 percent; two extra nights by 5 percent; and three or more nights by 4 percent

- Have incomes of $48,000 or more, compared with $37,000 for those who did not make heritage tours

- Be college graduates (41 percent, compared with 32 percent of those who did not include cultural/heritage sites) and in managerial or professional occupations (31 percent versus 24 percent of those who did not take cultural/heritage trips)

- Be married (67 percent, compared with 61 percent of those who did not take cultural/heritage excursions)

Like those travelers who did not include cultural/historic events in their trips, 50 percent were men and 50 percent were women. About half had children under age 18 still in the home.

In 1997 *A Profile of Travelers Who Participate in Historic and Cultural Activities,* the TIA's first-ever national study of the historical and cultural travel market, found that cultural and historic travelers:

- Spent, on average, $615 per trip, compared with $425 for other travelers

- Stayed in hotels, motels, or bed and breakfast inns more often (56 percent versus 42 percent of general travel population)

- Stayed an average of 4.7 nights, compared with 3.3 nights for all travelers

- Were more likely to include shopping on their trip (45 percent versus 33 percent)

- Were more likely to take group tours (7 percent versus 3 percent)

The TIA reported that June, July, and August were the most popular months for cultural and historic travel. Heritage/cultural visitors were most likely to visit California, New York, Pennsylvania, Texas, and Virginia. Also popular were Florida, North Carolina, Tennessee, Illinois, Georgia, and Ohio.

Consumer interest has led many corporate sponsors to invest in programs promoting heritage tourism. Travel services companies have invested in projects by the National Trust for Historic Preservation to help communities develop their historic and cultural sites. Some hotels and car rental agencies have contributed to education programs for children regarding historic sites across the United States.

The National Trust for Historic Preservation reported that motorcoach travelers, who were primarily 65 and older, led to the greatest increase in traffic at their historic sites. Sixty-eight percent of sites named motorcoach travelers as a growth market for them, while 50 percent named student groups; 46 percent, families; and 45 percent, seniors (sites could name more than one group).

Civil War Reenactments—Mock Combat

A growing number of people now participate in reenactments of the U.S. Civil War. Estimates as to the number of these hobbyists varied. In 1996 a reenactment of the Battle of Antietam drew 13,000 costumed people to Maryland. In 1997 almost 20,000 costumed soldiers and civilians met on the fields of Gettysburg for the 134th anniversary of that battle. The *Camp Chase Gazette,* a trade publication, estimated that there were between 20,000 and 25,000 active Civil War reenactors. When they attend a reenactment, they often bring their families along with them.

Reenactors visit school classrooms, march in parades, teach seminars, and hold public demonstrations, in addition to weekend battle games. Groups also meet in a number of overseas countries, including England, Germany, Taiwan, France, Belgium, Spain, Japan, Sweden, and Norway. The hobby has also spread to areas of the country that never experienced the war. About one hundred reenactment groups have Internet sites. In California, the American Civil War Association grew from six member groups in 1995 to five hundred in 1998. One of the biggest groups was based in Nashville, Tennessee—the North-South Alliance—which included the 3,500-member 1st Federal Division and the 5,000-member 1st Confederate Division.

Reenactments began in the 1960s at the time of the Civil War's centennial. A love of history and a desire to educate were the top motivations mentioned by reenactors. Interest in reenactments often grows after mass-market films are shown on television or at the movies.

Civil War reenactments are not for everyone. Just getting started requires buying period clothes, boots, a tent, mess equipment, and a gun, at a cost of $1,000–1,500. The cost can reach $2,000 for members of groups that are sticklers for authenticity. Those latter groups do not allow modern speech or eyeglasses. An estimated two hundred businesses have grown to satisfy the need for authenticity in costumes, including "great coats" and brogans, and equipment. The hobby also is not kind to older men. The average age of soldiers fell from 25 in 1862 to 18 in 1864. Also, marching long distances in inclement weather is often too physically demanding for older participants.

ROMANTIC VACATIONS

Many Americans enjoy romantic getaways, trips with a spouse or other love interest without children to rekindle romantic feelings in the relationship. According to the 1998 *TIA Travel Poll,* 31 percent (61.8 million) of American adults said they had taken a romantic vacation in the previous year. The average annual number of romantic getaways was 2.5. Among those people who took a romantic trip, 51 percent took one trip, and 26 percent took two trips in the previous year. One in 10 took five or more romantic vacations.

Not surprisingly, Americans without children in their households took more romantic vacations than parents of children (3.1 versus 1.9 trips, respectively). While on a romantic getaway, most travelers enjoyed visiting distant cities for dining and entertainment (74 percent). Forty-four percent went to beaches or lakes, while 21 percent took gambling vacations. Golf/tennis (12 percent), cruising (12 percent), and skiing (7 percent) also were popular. (See Figure 7.6.)

Men (54 percent) were more likely than women (46 percent) to consider their vacation trips as romantic getaways. Romantic travelers were more likely to be married (78 percent) than people who did not take romantic getaways (59 percent), and had higher incomes ($67,000) than adults who did not take romantic trips ($45,000).

Honeymooners outspent the average traveler by more than three times. On average, they spent $1,402, while the average trip expenditure in 1994 for all travelers was $421.

SHOPPING TRIPS TO OUTLET MALLS

Outlet shopping malls are becoming major attractions for American travelers. According to the *TIA Travel Poll,* of travelers on trips of 100 miles or more away from home, 37 percent (55 million) of all leisure and business travelers visited a discount outlet mall in 1997. Of the visitors, 46 percent were men and 54 percent were women. One in 10 respondents cited the outlet-shopping trip as the primary reason for their trip. Most (79 percent) said it was the secondary reason, and 11 percent said it was not an

FIGURE 7.6

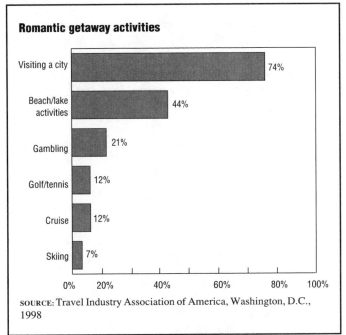

Romantic getaway activities

SOURCE: Travel Industry Association of America, Washington, D.C., 1998

FIGURE 7.7

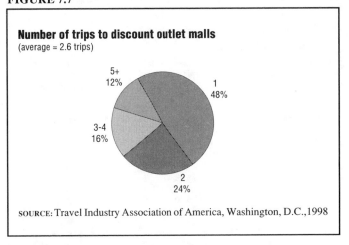

Number of trips to discount outlet malls
(average = 2.6 trips)

SOURCE: Travel Industry Association of America, Washington, D.C.,1998

original reason for the trip, although they did visit the malls. The travelers spent, on average, $183 at the malls.

One shopping trip in the previous year was taken by 48 percent of discount outlet shoppers; 12 percent took five or more shopping trips in the year. (See Figure 7.7.) On average, discount outlet travelers took 2.6 trips annually. Travelers of all ages, income levels, occupations, and marital status enjoyed discount outlet shopping.

FAMILY REUNIONS

Family reunions were popular with about one-third of all travelers, according to a 1997 *Better Homes and Gardens Family Vacation Travel Report.* Thirty-four percent of family vacationers—32 million travelers—attended a family reunion in 1996. Among different age groups, Generation X (18–34 years old) travelers were the most likely to attend a family reunion. The Midwest had the highest percentage of family reunion travelers, followed by the Northeast and the South.

COMBINING BUSINESS AND VACATION TRIPS

In 1996, according to the *1996 Survey of Business Travelers*—conducted by the TIA and the Official Airline Guides—8.8 million business travelers combined business and vacation on a trip, up from 7.5 million business travelers in 1994 and 6.5 million travelers in 1991. Nearly one-third (30 percent) of all business travel included some time for pleasure, and 36 percent of all business travel included an overnight weekend stay. Of those travelers, 53 percent were men, 47 percent were women, 65.7 percent were married, and 23.8 percent were single.

For dual-career couples, scheduling a vacation has become increasingly more difficult, and more people are combining business and pleasure. Hotels, therefore, are accommodating a growing number of people who are "on call" 365 days a year by providing fax machines and computer centers.

Executive Vacations

In 1998 Roper Starch, in *Spreadsheets to Sunshine: Executives on Vacation,* prepared for Hyatt Hotels and Resorts, surveyed 600 executives who had taken at least five consecutive days of vacation the previous year. The executives talked about what vacations meant to them. Almost 70 percent of the business executives reported that vacations were "essential" to their personal well-being, and 60 percent said vacations were vital to their job performance. (See Figure 7.8.)

Although time is money, most executives claimed they would rather have the vacation time than pay. Fully 70 percent would not sacrifice a week of paid vacation for a raise, although, surprisingly, half did not take all the vacation for which they were eligible. (See Figure 7.9.) Most men and older executives did not take all their vacation time; most women and younger executives did.

Although 7 in 10 executives said they were able to relax in the first two days of their weeklong vacation, 1 in 4 said work often interfered with their ability to enjoy the vacation. Eleven percent said their bosses made them feel guilty for taking their time off. Over half, 55 percent, spent part of their vacations dreaming about never returning to the "rat race." (See Figure 7.10.) Those daydreams were most common among the younger executives who had not attained the highest ranks.

Even when they were relaxing, most executives reported doing some work while on vacation. Three in four called the office, 71 percent checked their phone messages, 60 percent received e-mails or calls from the office, and 54 percent did some office work. (See Figure

FIGURE 7.8

Executives find vacations essential to their job performance and overall state of mind

"When it comes to maintaining a positive state of mind at work and keeping your job performance up, how important to you is taking a week-long vacation at least once a year? Would you say it is essential, important but not essential, not very important, or not important at all?"

"And when it comes to maintaining a positive state of mind in your personal life outside of work, how important to you is taking a week-long vacation at least once a year? Is it essential, important but not essential, not very important, or not important at all?"

Base: Total executives interviewed by telephone (N = 450).

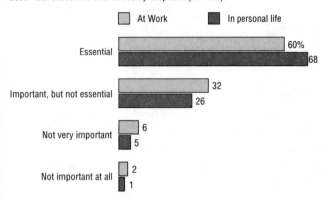

SOURCE: *Spreadsheets to Sunshine: Executives on Vacation*, prepared by Roper Starch for Hyatt Hotels & Resorts, Chicago, IL, 1998

FIGURE 7.9

Half of executives take fewer than their allowed vacation days per year

"In a typical year, how much of your allotted number of vacation days do you usually take? Would you say you take…"

Base: Total Executives Interviewed By Telephone (N = 450)

Number of allowed vacation days taken:

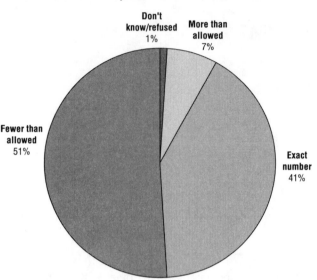

SOURCE: *Spreadsheets to Sunshine: Executives on Vacation*, prepared by Roper Starch for Hyatt Hotels & Resorts, Chicago, IL, 1998

FIGURE 7.10

On vacation, executives dream of escaping the "rat race"

"For each statement i read, please tell me if it describes you completely, somewhat, not much, or not at all. First …"

Base: Total executives interviewed by telephone (N = 450).

When I'm on vacation, I often dream about escaping the rat race

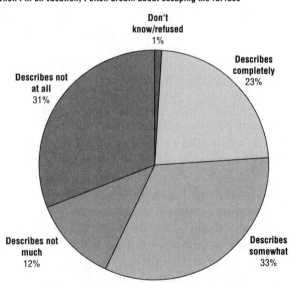

SOURCE: *Spreadsheets to Sunshine: Executives on Vacation*, prepared by Roper Starch for Hyatt Hotels & Resorts, Chicago, IL, 1998

FIGURE 7.11

Most executives have done some kind of office work while on vacation

"Again, while on vacation have you ever…"

Base: Total executives interviewed by telephone (N=450).

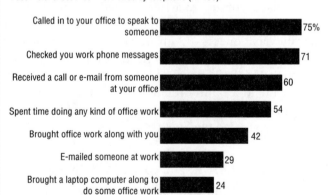

SOURCE: *Spreadsheets to Sunshine: Executives on Vacation*, prepared by Roper Starch for Hyatt Hotels & Resorts, Chicago, IL, 1998

FIGURE 7.12

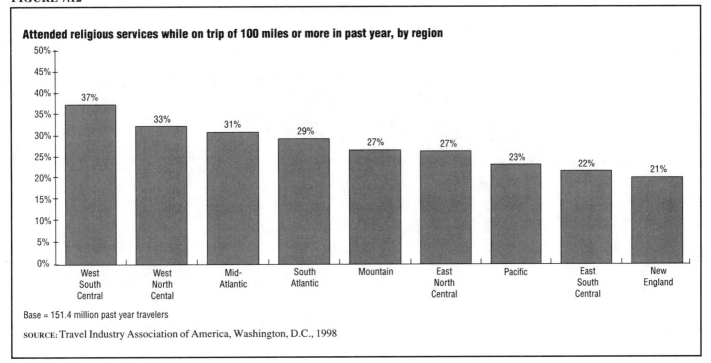

Attended religious services while on trip of 100 miles or more in past year, by region

Base = 151.4 million past year travelers

SOURCE: Travel Industry Association of America, Washington, D.C., 1998

7.11.) Vacation plans were canceled by 25 percent because of work "crises," and 14 percent cut their vacations short because of work-related emergencies. Forty percent of the executives kept track of the stock market while they were on vacation, and 20 percent read a daily business paper "religiously." (See Table 7.4.)

Nevertheless, 70 percent found time for romance with a "significant other" while on vacation. Sixty-four percent said they ate more than usual, and 47 percent reported drinking more than they usually did. More than half (53 percent) of the executives said they had sex more while on vacation than usual. A book was read for pleasure (all the way through) by 67 percent and 40 percent kept track of financial matters while they were gone. (See Table 7.4.)

Business travelers often take children on their trips. In 1997, 24.4 million business trips included a child, up significantly from the 7.4 million business trips that included a child in 1987. In addition, 17 percent of all business trips included two household members.

Business travelers enjoy their free time on the road. A 1995 survey by Novotel New York found that only 7 percent of those surveyed said they felt lonely while traveling. More men (26 percent) than women (18 percent) said they missed their families while on the road. For their favorite pastime while traveling, men preferred dinner, followed by rest, work, entertainment, sightseeing, shopping, and exercise. Businesswomen chose shopping over dinner, followed by exercise, then rest, work, and sightseeing. Sixty-six percent preferred to eat dinner outside the hotel. For women, their favorite way to relax in a hotel room was to talk on the phone; men preferred to have a drink.

TABLE 7.4

Other favorite activities

"While on vacation in the past 12 months have you ever . . ."

Base: Total executives interviewed by telephone. Percent who say "yes."

		Job title			
	Total	CEO/ Pres./ E or SVP	VP/ Dir.	Mgr./ Sup.	Sales Man./ Rep.
(Unweighted base)	(450) %	(47) %	(135) %	(230) %	(37) %
Read a book for pleasure all the way through	67	67	75	59	80
Checked how stocks, bonds or mutual bonds are doing	40	28	47	38	20
Played golf	35	33	42	29	60
Gone swimming	34	43	34	32	32
Taken a trip outside the US	33	61	33	26	40
Gambled at a casino	28	22	27	29	40
Gone walking, fitness walking	24	23	30	22	16
Gone snow skiing	21	22	25	17	20
Read a daily business paper religiously	20	28	18	18	40
Gone to a spa	18	17	18	18	20

SOURCE: *Spreadsheets to Sunshine: Executives on Vacation,* prepared by Roper Starch for Hyatt Hotels & Resorts, Chicago, IL, 1998

FIGURE 7.13

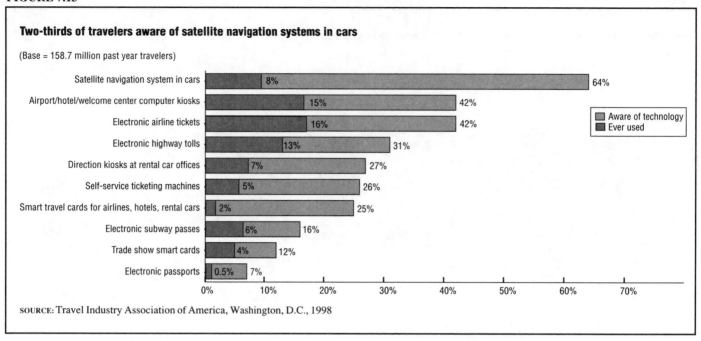

Two-thirds of travelers aware of satellite navigation systems in cars

(Base = 158.7 million past year travelers)

	Aware of technology	Ever used
Satellite navigation system in cars	64%	8%
Airport/hotel/welcome center computer kiosks	42%	15%
Electronic airline tickets	42%	16%
Electronic highway tolls	31%	13%
Direction kiosks at rental car offices	27%	7%
Self-service ticketing machines	26%	5%
Smart travel cards for airlines, hotels, rental cars	25%	2%
Electronic subway passes	16%	6%
Trade show smart cards	12%	4%
Electronic passports	7%	0.5%

SOURCE: Travel Industry Association of America, Washington, D.C., 1998

According to a 1999 report by the TIA, 197 million business trips were taken in 1998, an increase of 5 percent over 1997 figures. The average age of a business traveler rose from 40 in 1990 to 42 in 1998. The average income of business travelers in 1998 was $76,100. The percentage of business travelers in the health, legal, and educational services field increased from 19 percent in 1991 to 25 percent in 1998. The percentage of business travelers in professional/managerial occupations peaked in 1994 at 55 percent. Since then it has decreased, going down to 47 percent in 1998.

RELIGIOUS ATTENDANCE WHILE TRAVELING

In 1998 the TIA reported that 28 percent of adult travelers—43 million people—in the United States went to a church, temple, mosque, or other place of worship for a regularly scheduled religious service while on a trip of 100 miles or more in the past year. This did not include those travelers who went to a place of worship for sightseeing or for a special event, such as a wedding, funeral, confirmation, or bar mitzvah.

By region, residents of the West South Central (Texas, Oklahoma, Louisiana, and Arkansas) reported the highest attendance (37 percent), while residents in New England (Connecticut, Maine, Massachusetts, New Hampshire, Rhode Island, and Vermont) registered the lowest (21 percent). (See Figure 7.12.) Among the groups having high attendance were:

- Travelers aged 55–64 (41 percent)

- College graduates (39 percent)

- Retired travelers (32 percent)

Just over one-half (51 percent) of travelers who attended a religious service were accompanied by a spouse, and 38 percent had children or grandchildren with them. Fifteen percent traveled alone on the trip in which they attended religious services—24 percent on business trips, and 32 percent were retired.

ARRANGED TRIPS FOR THE OLDER GENERATION

Elderhostel, a nonprofit organization that arranges trips for people 55 and older, reported that it had grown from 240 participants in the 1980s to 10,000 programs attended by more than 300,000 people a year. Among the trips available to seniors were whale watching off Baja California, exploring American Indian culture at reservations, and dabbling in alternative healing in Montana.

TECHNOLOGY AND TRAVEL

The TIA reported, in its *Technology and Travel 1998,* that people who enjoyed the Internet also traveled a lot. Of Internet users, 92 percent took a trip of 100 miles or more away from home in the previous year. Forty-five percent of all Internet users were frequent travelers, those who took five or more trips in 1998.

The report also found that use of the Internet had grown dramatically since 1996. The number of travelers who used online services for travel-related purposes more than doubled from 29 million in 1996 to 70 million in 1998. The report also found that 48 percent of all online travelers and 51 percent of all frequent travelers consulted the Internet for information on destinations or to check prices and schedules.

Travelers were asked if they had heard of 10 new travel technologies, including satellite navigation systems, computer services in airports and hotels, electronic and self-service ticketing, "smart" cards, and electronic passports. Most (82 percent) had heard of at least one, and two out of five travelers (44 percent) had actually tried at least one. Seventy-one percent would consider trying the technologies in the future. (Figure 7.13 shows the percentages of people who were aware of and had used various new travel technologies.)

The Internet has come to play a role in planning travel and vacations as well. A June 2000 report by the TIA found that of those surveyed, 21 percent used the Internet to plan their vacation. (See Table 7.5.) Only newspapers were used more often.

Among those who used more than one medium, however, the Internet ranked number one in usefulness. Clearly, the role played by the Internet in travel will continue to grow.

WORLD TOURISM

Global tourism and travel more than doubled in the 1990s as the standard of living for many people in the world rose and more countries became accessible to tourists. In 1997, according to the World Tourism Organization (WTO), the world's top tourist destinations (in millions of arrivals) were France (66.8), the United States (48.9), Spain (43.4), Italy (34), the United Kingdom (26), China (23.7), Poland (19.5), Mexico (18.6), Canada (17.5), and the Czech Republic (17.4). Tourists spent $447.7 billion in 1997, up from $315.5 billion in 1992 and $204.7 billion in 1988.

The WTO predicted in its *Tourism 2020 Vision Executive Summary* that China would likely be the top destination for international travel in 2020. The agency projected that China, excluding Hong Kong, would receive 137.1 million visitors, while Hong Kong would receive 59.3 million. The United States, the second-most popular future

TABLE 7.5

Mediums used in 1999 to plan a trip or vacation*

Newspaper travel section	28%
Internet Web site	21%
Travel show on television or cable	21%
Motor Club Magazine, such as AAA	18%
Consumer lifestyle magazines	17%
News magazines	12%
Consumer travel magazine	12%
Membership publication	12%
Travel guidebook	11%
In-flight magazine from an airline	10%
A travel trade or business publication	10%
An electronic or e-mail newsletter	9%

Multiple responses allowed

SOURCE: "New Survey on Travel Media finds that Internet Travel Sites are Most Useful to Travelers.," *TIA Travel Poll,* Travel Industry Association of America, Washington, D.C., June 12, 2000

destination point, would receive 102.4 million visitors in 2020. France would get 93.3 million visits, followed by Spain, with 71 million. China (8 percent) would experience the largest rate of increase annually; U.S. arrivals were expected to grow an average of 3.5 percent per year.

Outbound Tourism from the United States

About half the trips that Americans make to foreign locations are to Canada and Mexico. According to the WTO, in 1997, 21.6 million U.S. resident travelers went to overseas destinations (which does not include Mexico and Canada), averaging 3.2 trips over the previous 12 months. The locations most frequently visited included the United Kingdom (17 percent), France (10 percent), Germany (8 percent), Italy (7 percent), and Jamaica (6 percent). The top activities for U.S. travelers abroad were dining in restaurants (85 percent), shopping (76 percent), visiting historical sites (53 percent), sightseeing in cities (44 percent), and visiting small towns/villages (44 percent). Americans traveling abroad spent an estimated $54.4 million in 1998, up from $43.9 million in 1992.

CHAPTER 8
THE ROLE OF RECREATION IN AMERICAN SOCIETY

A CHANGING ROLE

The expectations of free time have expanded. Eric Miller, in *At Our Leisure* (1992), portrayed recreation and leisure in the United States in the 1950s as an expression of comfort; it rounded out lives and reaffirmed the importance of home and family. In the 1960s, it acquired an identity of its own apart from "traditional values." In the 1970s, free time became an expression of a person's identity; it pushed work into secondary importance. In the 1980s, Americans began to work at having fun—it was an opportunity to claim the rewards of one's labor.

Americans spent wildly on material necessities, pleasures, and extravagances. Shopping became a form of recreation; American leisure included unabashed consumerism. At the turn of the twenty-first century, Americans have demanded more of their free time—recreation now must provide personal satisfaction. As people begin to recognize there is a limit to the quantity of life, they have turned their attention to the quality of their lives.

American culture's structuring of leisure is relatively new. The five-day workweek was institutionalized as a part of President Franklin Roosevelt's New Deal (1938), and Americans settled into "9-to-5" (or slight variations) workdays after World War II. When free time became a national institution, no corresponding leisure industry existed. Since then, leisure has developed into a huge industry. According to the U.S. Department of Labor, in 1996 Americans spent 5.4 percent of their annual expenditures on entertainment, nearly equal to the 5.2 percent they spent on health care.

Looking for Fulfillment

The work world has changed greatly. More and more people work in structured, hierarchical environments. Many perform very specialized, repetitive tasks. Many workers report they are fulfilled less than previously by the actual work they do—they feel less creative, and they say they have little input. Some workers report their jobs involve constant monitoring and little or no autonomy. In addition, employees often feel they lack job security or loyalty from their employers. Employers frequently fire, downsize, or lay off workers.

Consequently, studies have suggested that many workers derive satisfaction from their jobs today primarily based on external factors: they are pleased with their salaries or they are grateful for their benefit and health packages. In such a situation, recreation takes on added importance to the overall happiness of a person's life.

Many of the most popular forms of recreation are popular for three reasons: they are convenient, possible to do alone or with others, and able to be done for pleasure instead of competition. For example, treadmills, resistance machines, and other indoor activities are popular because they can be done almost anywhere, anytime, alone or with another person.

A Style of Socializing

Many forms of recreation are popular because they are done with other people—they are a way of socializing. Many young people enjoy sports as an inexpensive dating practice, believing they can get to know another person well from going in-line skating or bicycling together. Billiards in smoke-free, upscale parlors has become a "hip" couples' activity. Bowling has once again become popular. Many tout health clubs and sporting activities as great ways to meet persons of the opposite sex.

Other activities are popular because health professionals recommend them. In a very health-conscious society, many people are working out with weights, men primarily for strengthening their bodies, women to combat osteoporosis, and both sexes to lose weight.

A CHANGING MARKET

The gaming industry reported, in its *International Gaming and Wagering Business* magazine ("Boomers Are a Tough Target," May 1998), that, as in many entertainment industries, the next wave of mega-resorts and vacation destinations will have to target a new group: the affluent baby boomer. Some of the most important trends include:

- Boomers will demand holistic experiences—locations that allow them to nurture their mind, body, and spirit. Learning will increasingly be part of the vacation experience.

- Vacation resorts will have to offer entertainment for the whole family. In two-income families, parents will consider vacations as a way of reconnecting with children rather than escaping them, as in the past.

- Authenticity is important. People will visit places that are fabricated once because they are new and exciting, but they will not often return. Visitors will seek locations that are genuine in a particular setting—a cabin in the woods or at the seashore, for example.

- Boomers want things to be hassle-free. In their already complicated lives, they will seek vacations that are well-programmed so that they can enjoy them and do not have to think.

- Technology will be essential to a boomer getaway. If boomers can work while on their vacation, they will stay longer. They will need modems and business services on the premises. Many will consider a vacation hotel an extension of their office.

In order to survive, leisure activities and vacation destinations will have to evolve to retain the changing market.

SPORTS—AN EXPRESSION OF NATIONAL VALUES

A Brief History of American Sports

From ancient times, sports helped define manhood. Powerful men displayed their status and wealth by building horse-racing tracks or sponsoring sporting events, while humbler ones gained a sense of masculinity, and sometimes wealth, as participants or spectators in games. According to recent interpretation, despite differences in social rank, sports united men in a shared patriarchal culture. Athletics encouraged men to display their competitiveness and physical abilities and encouraged them to think in terms of winning and losing. Sports generally helped build a vision of masculinity that emphasized aggression and physicality.

In the late 1800s the advent of daily sports pages and telegraph lines to transmit baseball results contributed to a growing sporting culture. The expansion of cities spurred the growth of sports, which developed most rapidly in urban areas, where a growing manufacturing economy was producing huge amounts of wealth. As cities grew, recreation was increasingly transformed into entertainment, an amusement to be purchased with earnings.

Despite events that drew many thousands of fans and hundreds of newspaper reporters, professionalism in sports was still unusual, profits were secondary to pleasure, organizations were informal, and scheduling was irregular. Sports continued to be voluntary associations based on class, ethnic, or occupational background. Sports, like religion, politics, and business, were a glue holding diverse Americans together.

Not only were sports changing and growing, many Americans were beginning to see sports as a moral force. Taking charge of one's physical condition became a prerequisite for a virtuous, self-reliant, spiritually elevated life. Moral improvement, self-mastery, and godliness were invoked in the name of sports. By the mid-1800s, even clergymen, intellectuals, and reformers "took up the cause." As Henry David Thoreau declared, "The body existed for the highest development of the soul."

The Profit Motive Emerges—Professionalization and Commercialization

In an era of urban overcrowding and strict labor discipline, leisure activities could blunt a worker's rebelliousness. Reformers argued that sports refreshed workers' spirits, improved their productivity, and alleviated class tensions. And the claim began to be heard that sports built character. Other people found they could earn money for teaching a game or by hustling other players.

Sports became part of a new consumerism. New technologies led to better sports gear and equipment, and as a result, improved performance. A sports team became an employer with a "bottom line." Unlike those who earlier participated because they believed it could improve their body or their character, players now threw a ball to earn a living. Sports had become big business. Those who did not compete in sports could pay to see other people compete.

Salaries in Sports

And pay they do. During the 1998–99 season, the average price of tickets to watch a football game ranged from $33.99 in St. Louis to $74.99 in Washington, D.C. A ticket to see the New York Knicks play in Madison Square Garden averaged nearly $80. A ticket to see the New York Rangers play in the same venue averaged $58.83. Of the major sports, major league baseball tickets remained the most affordable. The average price to see a major league baseball game ranged from $8.46 in Minnesota to $24.05 in Boston's Fenway Park.

As the twenty-first century begins, everyone recognizes that sports are commercial endeavors. As employers, sports teams pay their players some of the highest salaries earned in the United States. During 1998, Deion Sanders, a cornerback with the Dallas Cowboys, reportedly was paid $7.5 million to play football. So was Dan Marino, a quarterback for the Miami Dolphins. Seven football players were paid more than $5 million that year.

Baseball players did even better. Albert Belle, a left fielder for Baltimore, was paid nearly $12 million. Pedro Martinez, a pitcher for Boston, was paid $11 million. The top 10 most highly paid baseball players all made at least $9 million. In December 2000, the Texas Rangers signed shortstop Alex Rodriguez to a 10-year contract reportedly worth $252 million. This is more than a quarter of a billion dollars being paid for someone to play baseball.

Pro basketball players, too, did extremely well during the 1998–99 season. Kevin Garnett reportedly received $21 million. Shaquille O'Neal was paid more than $17 million by Los Angeles. Patrick Ewing was paid almost as much by the New York Knicks. The 10 most highly paid basketball players all received at least $11 million during 1998–99. In the National Basketball Association (NBA), the average salary of a player was $2.5 million.

Sports are Big Business

Street & Smith's Sports Business Journal asked researchers to estimate the value of the sports industry. The estimate was $213 billion. This is almost as much as the banking industry, at $266 billion. A January 2000 report estimated networks paid the National Football League $2.27 billion to broadcast football; the NBA $660 million to broadcast basketball; and the NCAA $564 million to broadcast its events.

Advertising

Sports events draw huge crowds and receive media coverage unlike almost any other events. Advertising for sports events—and for other products at sports events—is enormous. A 30-second commercial advertisement played during the 2000 Super Bowl game cost about $2 million, up from $1.6 million in 1999. The advertisers pay these tremendous fees because the Super Bowl is one of the most-watched shows on television.

Sports stars also cash in on advertising. Many stars receive enormous sums of money to endorse products. Some question the message that this sends to children who look to sports figures as role models.

Amateur Sports

Just like professional sports, even amateur sports are big business. Some critics believe that the status of amateur sports, even down to the high school and junior high level, is threatened. They cite scandals involving recruiting, redshirting (the practice of holding a player back a year until he grows bigger, gets better, or a player in his position graduates; although the player attends school, he does not use up a year of athletic eligibility), phony courses, bogus grades, and payola. Professional and Olympic sports often suffer scandals involving steroid and drug use, sexual misconduct, and corruption.

Looking Good

When Americans participate in a sports activity, they often buy the best equipment and gear. A healthy economy has enabled many Americans to have a considerable amount of discretionary income, and much of that goes to support their varied sports and fitness interests. Your neighbor might run only 3 miles a week, but she can look professional by wearing the same equipment as a professional marathoner who runs 150 miles a week. Sporting goods is a thriving market, with new technologies and products arriving on the shelves weekly. Very often, when Americans buy a sports or recreation item, it is the most expensive version. For example, motorcycle and RV dealers reported that the largest growth in their product lines was in the best-equipped, "high end" items.

Many Americans not only participate in a sport or fitness activity: increasingly they compete against others. While many people still jog or run for health, many do so competitively—in marathons. A biker may not necessarily ride his bike to the grocery store, but he may enter (with a racing bike costing thousands of dollars) bike races or weekend group rides. Some take biking holidays, riding a tour bus from place to place and taking biking day trips.

National Values

Labor and play once blended into each other more freely than today because leisure time and work time were not so rigidly segmented. Moreover, sports were not necessarily played according to standardized rules—they were often a part of local culture, passed on by word of mouth, with rules varying from place to place. Today's sports include layers of communication, transportation, professionalism, regulating bodies, records, statistics, and media coverage.

Sports are very much a part of American values. It would be very easy to confuse a Super Bowl presentation with a Fourth of July celebration, with its veneration of nationalism, racial and ethnic integration, "rugged individualism," and hard work. Yet, some see the Super Bowl as not just a big game, but as a cynical manipulation of the American people to sell advertisements and make owners, players, and television networks rich.

Violence in the Sports Arena

Although physical prowess has a place in American society today, it competes with an appreciation of and need for other qualities, such as intellect and cooperation. And physical aggressiveness, in a civil society, sometimes

TABLE 8.1

What man or woman living anytime this century do you think was the greatest athlete of the century, in terms of their athletic performance?

Michael Jordan	23%
Muhammad Ali	9
Babe Ruth	4
Jim Thorpe	4
Jesse Owens	3
Walter Payton	2
Jackie Joyner-Kersee	2
Wayne Gretzky	1
Babe Didrikson Zaharias	1
Florence Griffith Joyner	1
Mark McGwire	1
Joe Montana	1
Carl Lewis	1
Pete Rose	1
Joe DiMaggio	1
Hank Aaron	1
Joe Louis	1
Bruce Jenner	1
Other	16
No opinion	26

Note: Results based on first mention.

SOURCE: *The Gallup Poll Monthly,* The Gallup Organization, Princeton, NJ, January 4, 2000

TABLE 8.2

In your opinion, who is the greatest athlete active in the world of sports today?

2000 Aug 24-27	%
Tiger Woods	30
Michael Jordan	4
Mark McGwire	3
Cal Ripken Jr.	2
Shaquille O'Neal	1
Brett Favre	1
Kobe Bryant	1
Sammy Sosa	1
Troy Aikman	1
Lance Armstrong	1
Pete Sampras	1
Venus Williams	1
Michael Johnson	1
Deion Sanders	1
Ken Griffey Jr.	1
Dale Earnhardt	1
Cynthia Cooper	1
Other	13
None	4
Don't know	30
No opinion	1
Total	100%

SOURCE: *The Gallup Poll Monthly,* The Gallup Organization, Princeton, NJ, August 31, 2000

presents serious problems. When people are trained and encouraged to be physically aggressive, they sometimes seem unable to harness those tendencies outside the sports arena. Hitting an opponent so hard that he has trouble getting up is a positive act loudly applauded on the playing field; do it in the parking lot after the game and an athlete—or spectator—can go to jail.

The Deification of Sports Figures—Who Are the Heroes?

The sudden flowering of a "mass culture" brought about by the growth in media and communications produced a wealth of new sports heroes. Increasingly, the public world became populated by sports celebrities with national reputations and appeal—heroes, such as Joe Louis, Jackie Robinson, Babe Didrikson Zaharias, Muhammad Ali, Joe DiMaggio, Babe Ruth, Sandy Koufax, and Billie Jean King.

The Gallup organization conducted a survey and reported in January 2000 that Michael Jordan, by an enormous margin, was considered to be the top athlete of the twentieth century. A sampling of adults, aged 18 and older, were asked "what man or woman living anytime this century do you think was the greatest athlete of the century, in terms of their athletic performance?" Michael Jordan was chosen by 23 percent. (See Table 8.1.) The next closest athlete was boxer Muhammad Ali with 9 percent. Other athletes chosen who received as much as 2 percent of the vote were Babe Ruth (4 percent), Jim Thorpe (4 percent), Jesse Owens (3 percent),

Walter Payton (2 percent), and Jackie Joyner-Kersee (2 percent).

Another Gallup poll reported in August 2000 that 3 in 10 Americans believed that Tiger Woods was the greatest athlete active in the world of sports today. (See Table 8.2.) The only other sport figures receiving more than 1 percent of the votes were Michael Jordan (4 percent), Mark McGwire (3 percent), and Cal Ripken Jr. (2 percent).

Are They What They Seem?

Such sports celebrities became a potential powerful force in society that could be marketed. The growing professions of advertising and public relations began to link these icons to products. The public's fascination with fame and glamour enabled heroes to mold the taste of their fans. Sports heroes have generally become marketing images rather than real human beings.

As a result, many people have come to revere sports figures, to regard them as heroes, and to credit them with attributes they may not possess. The American public holds its sports figures in high esteem, puts them on pedestals, and appears truly shocked when heroes demonstrate they are mortals who share the weaknesses of others. Although sports have always had their share of misbehavior, in recent years the media has been able to publicize the indiscretions of a number of sports figures. Famous athletes, when viewed as role models, have sometimes disappointed and disenchanted admiring fans.

RECREATION FOR HEALTH

Americans are living longer and are generally healthier. More people are able physically and, increasingly, financially to participate in recreational activities. As likely as not, the biker riding a Harley is someone with gray hair. The men and women playing softball may well all be over 65. Older consumers are a growing market in the sales of many consumer items, including recreation vehicles, sporting goods, books, and computers.

RECREATION FOR HEALING—RECREATIONAL THERAPY

Ancient teachings are replete with claims of the benefits of recreational experiences: "A merry heart doeth good like a medicine" (Proverbs) and "You can learn more about a man in an hour of play than in a lifetime of conversation" (Plato). But beginning in the nineteenth century, such principles began to be applied in health-care settings in a purposeful, organized manner.

Increasingly, medical experts are applying recreation to healing. Therapists currently are studying the effects of aquatic therapy on the treatment of multiple sclerosis (MS). Others have found that horseback riding, for unknown reasons, produces a remission in some MS patients. Mental health facilities now recognize the importance of bright, healthy surroundings and pleasant diversions for sufferers of mental and emotional conditions, unlike the harsh penal atmosphere generally accorded to patients in early mental facilities.

Many people have found that the presence of animals helps the recovery of the ill and improves the conditions of patients in nursing homes. Some studies have documented the improvement in blood pressure from simply observing an aquarium. Almost everyone understands that doing something pleasant is good for one's overall health.

As the sea of baby boomers reaches retirement age, a time that often includes the onset of physical disorders, many will use recreational therapy to help them not only to cope with, but also to heal from illness. These baby boomers are healthier, more active, and more affluent than previous generations, exactly the qualities that will likely lead them to seek recreational therapies.

IMPORTANT NAMES AND ADDRESSES

American Theatre
Theatre Communications Group
355 Lexington Ave.
New York, NY 10017
(212) 697-5230
FAX (212) 983-4847
URL: http://www.tcg.org

Association of American Publishers
71 Fifth Ave.
New York, NY 10003-3004
(212) 255-0200
FAX (212) 255-7007
URL: http://www.publishers.org

Association of Racing Commissioners International
2343 Alexandria Dr., Suite 200
Lexington, KY 40504
(859) 224-7070
FAX (859) 224-7071
URL: http://www.arci.com

Book Industry Study Group, Inc.
160 Fifth Ave.
New York, NY 10010-7000
(212) 929-1393
FAX (212) 989-7542
URL: http://www.bisg.org

Consumer Electronics Association
2500 Wilson Blvd.
Arlington, VA 22201
(703) 907-7600
FAX (703) 907-7675
URL: http://www.ce.org

Hobby Industry Association
P.O. Box 348
Elmwood Park, NJ 07407
(201) 794-1133
FAX (201) 797-0657
URL: http://www.hobby.org

Motion Picture Association of America
15503 Ventura Blvd.
Encino, CA 91436
(818) 995-6600
URL: http://www.mpaa.org

Motorcycle Industry Council
2 Jenner St., Suite 150
Irvine, CA 92618
(949) 727-4211
FAX (949) 727-4217

Museum of Television and Radio
25 W. 52nd Ave.
New York, NY 10019
(212) 621-6600
FAX (212) 621-6700
URL: http://www.mtr.org

National Collegiate Athletic Association
700 W. Washington St.
P.O. Box 6222
Indianapolis, IN 46206-6222
(317) 917-6222
FAX (317) 917-6888
URL: http://www.ncaa.org

National Endowment for the Arts
1100 Pennsylvania Ave. NW, Room 720
Washington, D.C. 20506-0001
(202) 682-5400
FAX (202) 682-5447
URL: http://arts.endow.gov

National Marine Manufacturers Association
200 E. Randolph Dr., Suite 5100
Chicago, IL 60601
(312) 946-6200
FAX (312) 946-0388
URL: http://www.nmma.org

National Park Service
1849 C St. NW
Washington, D.C. 20240

(202) 208-6843
FAX (202) 219-0910
URL: http://www.nps.gov

National Sporting Goods Association
1601 Feehanville Dr., Suite 300
Mt. Prospect, IL 60056-6035
(847) 296-6742
FAX (847) 391-9827
URL: http://www.nsga.org

National Trust for Historic Preservation
1785 Massachusetts Ave. NW
Washington, D.C. 20036
(202) 588-6000
FAX (202) 588-6223
URL: http://www.nthp.org

Newspaper Association of America
1921 Gallows Rd., Suite 600
Vienna, VA 22182-3900
(703) 902-1600
FAX (703) 902-1800
URL: http://www.naa.org

Recording Industry Association of America
1330 Connecticut Ave. NW, Suite 300
Washington, D.C. 20036
(202) 775-0101
FAX (202) 775-7253
URL: http://www.riaa.com

The Recreation Roundtable
1225 New York Ave. NW
Washington, D.C. 20005
(202) 682-9530
FAX (202) 682-9529
URL: http://www.funoutdoor.com

Recreational Vehicle Industry Association
1896 Preston White Dr.
Reston, VA 20195
(703) 620-6003
FAX (703) 620-5071
URL: http://www.rvia.org

Sporting Goods Manufacturers Association
200 Castlewood Dr.
N. Palm Beach, FL 33418
(561) 842-4100
FAX (561) 863-8984
URL: http://www.sportlink.com

Toy Manufacturers of America
1115 Broadway, Suite 400
New York, NY 10010
(212) 675-1141
FAX (212) 633-1429
URL: http://www.toy-tma.org

Travel Industry Association of America
1100 New York Ave. NW, Suite 450
Washington, D.C. 20005-3934

(202) 408-8422
FAX (202) 408-1255
URL: http://www.tia.org

U.S. Department of Labor
Office of Public Affairs
200 Constitution Ave. NW, Room S-1093
Washington, D.C. 20210
(202) 693-4650
URL: http://www.dol.gov

U.S. Fish and Wildlife Service
U.S. Department of the Interior
1849 C St. NW, Room 3012
Washington, D.C. 20240-0001
(202) 208-4717
URL: http://www.fws.gov

U.S. Forest Service
U.S. Department of Agriculture
Sidney R. Yates Federal Building
201 14th St. SW
Washington, D.C. 20250
(202) 205-1661
URL: http://www.fs.fed.us

U.S. Travel and Tourism
Tourism Industries
U.S. Department of Commerce
1401 Constitution Ave. NW, Room 2073
Washington, D.C. 20230
(202) 482-2000
URL: http://www.tinet.ita.doc.gov

RESOURCES

The U.S. Department of Transportation periodically conducts its *American Travel Survey* on the travel of Americans. The U.S. Travel and Tourism Administration of the U.S. Department of Commerce keeps account of travel within the United States and overseas travel to and from the United States. The Travel Industry Association of America also generously provided information on travel by Americans, including the number of trips, the activities during trips, and demographic information about American travelers.

The National Park Service of the U.S. Department of the Interior published the *1997 Statistical Abstract,* with helpful information about the national parks, their facilities, the services they provide, the accommodations, the hours of operation, and the cost. The U.S. Fish and Wildlife Service of the U.S. Department of the Interior published the *1996 National Survey of Fishing, Hunting, and Wildlife-Associated Recreation.*

The U.S. General Accounting Office (GAO) monitors governmental activity and prepares briefing reports on various topics. The GAO report *Difficult Choices Need to Be Made about the Future of the Parks* (1995) was used in the preparation of this book. The International Association of Amusement Parks and Attractions provided helpful information on amusement parks and other attractions.

The National Endowment for the Arts provided important information on the trends in attendance of performing arts, motion pictures, and spectator sports during 1993-99. The Stanford Institute for the Qualitative Study of Society provided important information from its research on the Internet. The Book Industry Study Group and the American Booksellers Association shared the results of their research on America's reading and book-buying habits.

The Toy Manufacturers of America reports on the toy industry in its *Toy Industry Fact Book.* This annual report provides an overview of the toy industry and product safety, as well as marketing and advertising. The Hobby Industry Association, in its *1996-97 Size of Craft/Hobby Industry Study* (1998) and *The HIA 1998 Nationwide Craft/Hobby Consumer Study* (1999), supplied information on hobbies, crafts, and collecting.

The National Sporting Goods Association provided important information on the sporting goods market and participation in sports, such as exercise walking, fishing, football, baseball, basketball, bicycle riding, bowling, and running. The Gale Group extends its appreciation to the National Collegiate Athletic Association for providing information on student athletes. The Sporting Goods Manufacturers Association supplied many useful publications and charts including *The Shifting Fashions in Exercise* (2000), *Recreational Sports: The Feminine Prerogative* (2000), and *Whassup...with Extreme Sports* (2000).

The Gale Group expresses its sincere appreciation to the Gallup Poll for several surveys used in this book and to Roper Starch Worldwide and Hyatt Hotels and Resorts for permission to use their *Spreadsheets to Sunshine: Executives on Vacation* (1998), which studied the attitudes of executives in two thousand of the nation's largest companies. The Gale Group is grateful for information from *International Gaming and Wagering Business*, a monthly trade magazine devoted to the gaming industry that contains invaluable data on every aspect of the industry and special reports on particular types of gambling activity, such as lotteries and casino gambling. Particularly helpful was its *U.S. Gross Annual Wager* (1997). The National Gambling Impact Study Commission's final report, issued on June 18, 1999, provided important information on the trends occurring in gambling in the United States.

The Gale Group would also like to thank the Association of Racing Commissioners International for permission to use material from its *Pari-mutuel Racing 1996—A*

Statistical Summary. Harrah's Survey of U.S. Casino Gaming Entertainment, developed by the NPD Group, identified American gambling preferences and habits.

The Gale Group is grateful for materials and information supplied by a number of private organizations and associations. Independent Sector's *America's Senior Volunteers*, *America's Teenage Volunteers*, and *America's Nonprofit Sector* provided data on volunteering in the United States. The Recreation Roundtable's *Outdoor Recreation in America 1999* provided invaluable information on participation in sports in the United States. Cruise Lines International Association provided information on cruises.

The Gale Group appreciates data on heritage and historical tourism received from the National Trust for Historic Preservation. The Pew Research Center allowed The Gale Group to use its *Internet News Takes Off* (1998), a study of American media use. The Recording Industry Association of America graciously permitted use of its *1999 Consumer Profile*. The Recreational Vehicle Industry Association provided valuable information, as did the Motorcycle Industry Council in its *Motorcycle Statistical Annual 1998*. The Consumer Electronics Association, too, provided valuable information for this publication.

UNIVERSITY H.S. LIBRARY

INDEX

7-18-03